Navigation of the Atlantic Ocean; with an account of the winds, weather and currents found therein ... Fourth and enlarged edition, etc.

Alexander Becher

Navigation of the Atlantic Ocean; with an account of the winds, weather and currents found therein ... Fourth and enlarged edition, etc.

Becher, Alexander
British Library, Historical Print Editions
British Library
1892
viii. 192 p. ; 8°.

The BiblioLife Network

GUIDE TO FOLD-OUTS, MAPS and OVERSIZED IMAGES

NAVIGATION

OF THE

[illegible]TLANTIC OCEAN.

[illegible]INDS, WEATHER, AND CURRENTS.

BY THE LATE

A. B. BECHER, CAPTAIN, R.N.

FIFTH EDITION.

LONDON:

PUBLISHED BY J. D. POTTER,

Sole Agent for the Sale of the Admiralty Charts,

[illegible] POULTRY, E.C., & 11, KING STREET, TOWER HILL, E.

PRICE FIVE SHILLINGS.

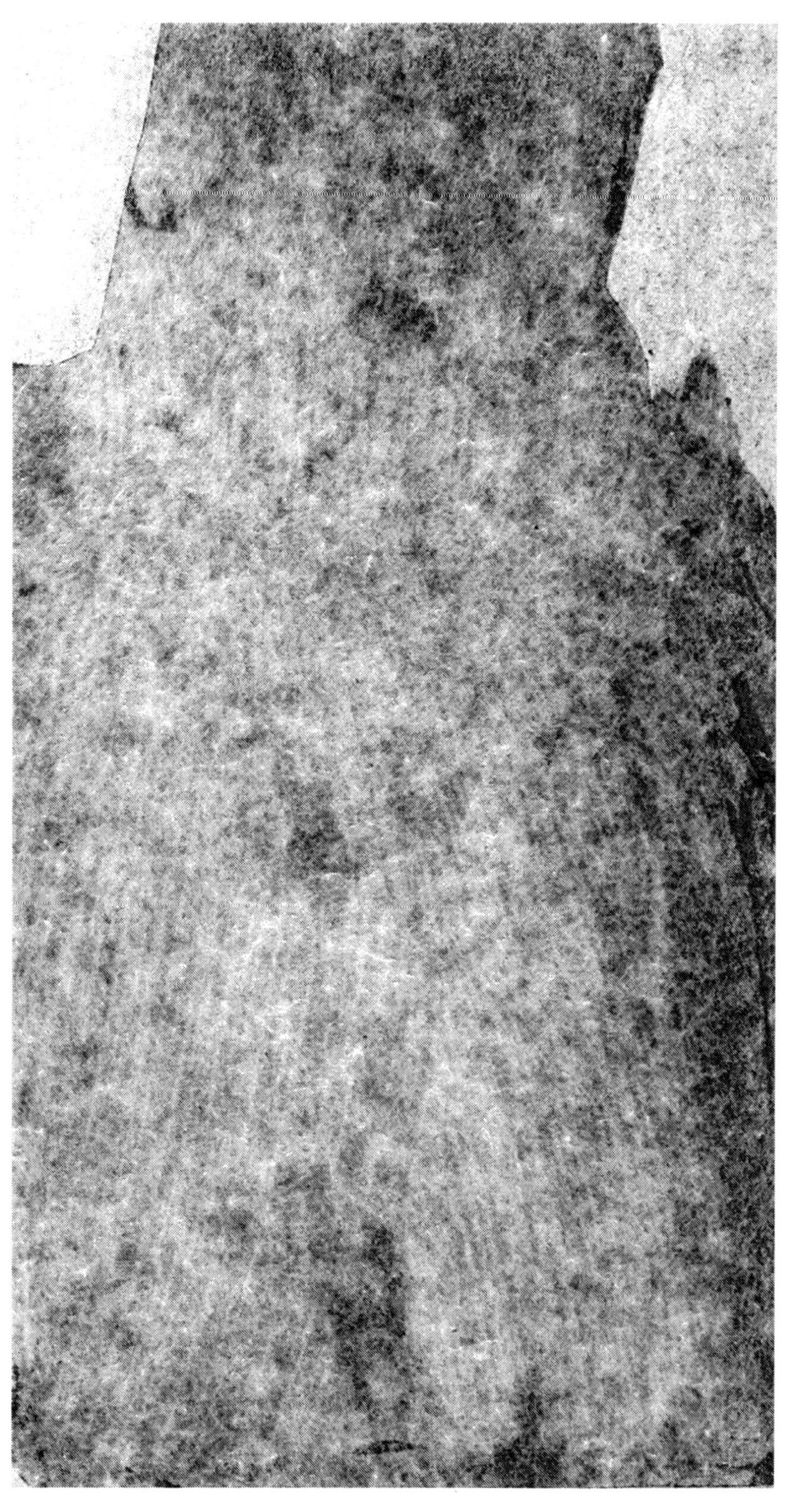

NAVIGATION

OF THE

ATLANTIC OCEAN;

WITH AN ACCOUNT OF THE

WINDS, WEATHER, AND CURRENTS

FOUND THEREIN THROUGHOUT THE YEAR;

ACCORDING TO THE MOST APPROVED AUTHORITIES, INCLUDING EXTENSIVE EXTRACTS FROM THE NAUTICAL MAGAZINE.

Fifth and Enlarged Edition.

WITH WIND AND CURRENT CHARTS.

That seamen may, with steam or sail,
Know where to meet the favoring gale;
May take instruction from the skies,
And find the path where swiftness lies.

BY (the late) A. B. BECHER, CAPTAIN, R.N.,

OF THE HYDROGRAPHIC OFFICE, ADMIRALTY,

Author of the Voyage of H.M.S. Chanticleer—The Landfall of Columbus—The Storm Compass—Editor and Author of various Papers in the Nautical Magazine.

London:

PUBLISHED BY J. D. POTTER,

Sole Agent for the Sale of the Admiralty Charts,

31, POULTRY, E.C., AND 11, KING STREET, TOWER HILL, E.

1892.

Price Five Shillings.

LONDON
GREAVES, PASS & CO., PRINTERS,
63, COLEMAN STREET, E.C.

THE

ATLANTIC OCEAN.

INTRODUCTION.

THE substance of the following pages is gathered from the valuable work of Captain KERHALLET, compiled from the voyages of the most celebrated navigators, and also contains information contributed to the NAUTICAL MAGAZINE by various commanders of our Mercantile Marine. It originally appeared in that periodical, and in its present form has passed through four editions. The ready manner in which these have been taken up affords good promise that this revised and enlarged edition will prove even more acceptable.

The subjects which it embraces are of much importance to the navigator; for, next to a fair wind, to know the season at the place to which he may be bound, how to go there, and when to go with regard to weather, is most desirable; and such is the object briefly treated in these pages.

Additions to this little work have been made from information derived from the voyages of recent navigators, the Admiralty Wind and Current Charts, and the records of the Meteorological Office.

CONTENTS.

THE
ATLANTIC OCEAN.

CHAPTER I.

General Winds: Theories of Origin and Cause—Torrid Zone—Trade Winds and their Limits—Deviation—Variable Winds—Seasons—The Frigid and Temperate Zones—Prevailing Winds of North and South Atlantic.

THE basin of the Atlantic Ocean (North and South), divided unequally between the West coasts of Europe and Africa and the East coast of America, presents a deep valley which appears bounded on the North and South only by the poles. Fields of ice have arrested the progress of navigators who have endeavoured to explore those regions.

In order to consider the winds common to this ocean, we shall divide it into three regions: the first, that comprised between the parallels of 30° North and South latitudes; the second, between the latitude of 30° South and the South pole: the third, between 30° North and the North pole. We shall divide each of these two last named regions into two zones; the temperate zone, extending from the parallel of 30° to 60°, and the frozen zone between the latitude of 60° and the poles.

We shall first consider the winds of each of these divisions of the ocean at a distance from the coast; and then, commencing at one extremity, shall describe the winds generally met with near the shore.

Origin and Causes of the Winds.—The winds owe their origin to all actions which disturb the equilibrium of the atmosphere. Science has endeavoured to determine the cause of wind and the general laws by which it is governed. Philosophers attribute winds to the heat of the sun, different and variable on the surface of the earth, in conjunction with the diurnal motion of the earth itself.

The differences between the temperature of the polar regions and of those near the equator being very great, they assert that there must, of necessity, be a constant change of air between these regions. Thus the cold and dense air of the polar regions tends to replace the warm and expanded air of the equatorial regions, which latter, rising and forming a higher current, should transfer itself towards the North and South, in order to restore the equilibrium.

If the earth were still, the winds on its surface would generally blow from North and South, according to the hemisphere in which they are; but the earth, turning from West to East on its axis, with a quickness which increases in proportion as the equator is neared; the consequence is, that in passing from high latitudes towards that great circle, currents of cold air arrive progressively in those regions where the rotatory motion is more considerable. Not being able to participate in this movement, on account of their want of cohesion with the earth, those winds take an opposite or inverted direction from that of the rotation of the globe, namely, from East to West.

Thus, the rotatory motion of the earth, combined with the different temperatures of the surface, causes the currents of air, coming from the North and South in each hemisphere, to deviate from their courses, and incline from the N.E. and S.E., producing the winds called the general or Trade winds of the torrid zone.

Without entering into the numerous theories on this subject, and the various objections to each, we shall confine ourselves to a statement of the leading authenticated facts regarding the winds of the Atlantic Ocean; the knowledge of which is of such vast importance to navigation.

North and South Polar Winds.—The two currents of air blowing from the North and South poles towards the equator as above mentioned, are termed polar winds, North or South, according to the hemisphere in which they are found.

North and South Tropical Winds.—On the contrary, those are called North and South tropical winds, which, from the equator, are directed towards the poles. These last appear to be counter-currents to the polar winds.

The Torrid Zone Trade Winds.—In the northern hemisphere, the polar winds blow from the N.E.; in the southern hemisphere from the S.E.; and they take a more easterly direction in proportion as they approach the equator. Between the tropics, these winds have received the more common name of "*Trade Winds* of each hemisphere." They are also called the "general winds of the torrid zone." These winds render the passage across the Atlantic from the Old to the New World, quick and easy.

The Trade winds appear to be the only primitive winds. Where they are established, the weather is always fine, and the sky generally clear. If they cease for awhile the sky becomes clouded, and, in certain parts, storms are experienced, the more lasting and severe in proportion as the places are more or less distant from the equator.

Those regions where the Trade winds do not prevail, are constantly exposed to stormy and tempestuous weather; where they cease from any cause, bad weather is experienced, and it has been remarked that they always return with some violent reaction, or with torrents of rain.

The Trade winds to the North and South of the equator have similar characters, as will be hereafter described.

Limits of the Trade Winds.—The polar limits of the Trade winds from N.E. and S.E. generally extend on each side of the equator to the parallels of 30° North and South latitude. Nevertheless this limitation differs greatly in some parts of the ocean, because it is influenced by temperature; and it varies about 3° North or South, according as the declination of the sun is North or South.

The equatorial limits of the N.E. and S.E. Trade winds are generally variable from the same causes. That of the N.E. Trade is about the mean parallel of 7° or 8° North latitude; that of the S.E. Trade is at the parallel of 2° or 3° North latitude.

From a numerous collection of observations, the following table has been formed: which, however, only affords an approximation to these limits:—

Month.	N.E. Trade Wind between 25° & 35° West.		S.E. Trade Wind between 20° & 30° West.	
	Equatorial Limit.	Polar Limit.	Equatorial Limit.	Polar Limit.
January	2° N.		2° N.	
February	1° N.	25° N.	1° 30′ N.	21° S.
March	0		1° N.	
April	1° N.		1° 30′ N.	
May	3° N.	28° N.	3° N.	23° S.
June	8° N.		4° 30′ N.	
July	10° N.		3° N.	
August	12° N.	29° N.	3° N.	23° S.
September	11° N.		1° 30′ N.	
October	10° N.		5° N.	
November	6° N.	25° N.	4° N.	13° S.
December	4° N.		3° N.	

In the Atlantic Ocean, the N.E. Trade wind in the part comprised between Cape Verd and the coast of Guinea, in the neighbourhood of the equator, has less force and constancy than that from the S.E.; owing, doubtless, to the form of the coasts which bound the ocean in this part. In the neighbourhood of the Antilles, it generally blows strongly, varying from East to N.E.

Peculiarities of the Trade Winds.—It has been observed, that in the zone comprised between the equator and the parallels of 28° North and South latitude, in proportion as the sun approaches the equator, the winds blow in the northern hemisphere almost from N.E., and in the southern hemisphere from S.E.

But if the sun has northern declination, and at its greatest distance from the equator, the winds in that hemisphere have a tendency to blow more from the East, and more violent storms are then experienced than at any other time. In the southern hemisphere the Trade wind then blows more from the South.

If, on the contrary, the sun has southern declination, the same facts are produced in an inverted order; thus, in this hemisphere the wind blows more from the East, while in the northern hemisphere it veers towards the North, and in this case they gain their nearest approach to the equator. And generally, in either zone, rain, sudden gusts of winds, and storms must be expected at those places where the sun is vertical.

Frequently the northern Trade is met near the latitude of Madeira. This fact is, however, only an exception to the general rule above laid down in alluding to the polar limit of this wind. At other times, the variable winds of the temperate zone extend to the southward as far as 20° North, without appearing subject to any general law; and this, too, in all seasons of the year.

In the southern hemisphere the case is much the

same. Thus, during the fine season, the southern limit of the S.E. Trade wind is found to be about the parallel of the Cape of Good Hope; while from June to August westerly winds are of frequent occurrence between that parallel and the tropic of Capricorn.

In the North Atlantic, at some distance from the coasts of Africa and America, a zone of calm and light variable winds is found between the northern limit of the N.E. Trade and about latitude 35° N.; the width varies according to the limit of the Trade wind. In this region the barometer is usually very high and steady.

In the South Atlantic a similar zone exists, but the calms are of much shorter duration.

Thus we see that the polar limits of the Trade winds are very variable. In the southern hemisphere this limit is sometimes near the tropic, but on the eastern side is more frequently on the parallel of the Cape of Good Hope.

In this same zone it has been observed, on the western side, that in latitude South of 16° S. the wind has a greater tendency to blow from the N.E. than from the S.E., so as to blow rather from East to N.E. than from East to S.E. This variation is also pretty frequent. During a year's stay at St. Helena, Halley found that, in that island, the Trade winds always blew from S.E. or nearly so; and that they more frequently veered from S.E. to East than from S.E. to South. During the East wind the weather was gloomy, and the return of fine weather depended on the wind from the S.E.

And, lastly, it may be stated that the polar limit of the N.E. Trade is found in a higher latitude on the eastern than on the western side, being influenced by the continent of Africa.

From the same cause the polar limit of the S.E. Trade is found as much as 10° more to the South on the African than on the American side.

Deviations in the Trade Winds.—It happens sometimes in the region of the Trade winds, that winds from opposite directions interrupt their usual course.* These winds are never of long duration, and only arise from accidental causes.

In the neighbourhood of the islands situated in the zone of the Trade wind, this wind is also interrupted. Thus, among the Cape Verd Islands, the N.E. Trade wind is often lost; and between the parallel of 10° latitude and the equator, from the meridian of Cape Verd to the most westerly meridian of this Archipelago, it is observed that there is, in reality, no settled wind,

* Columbus, who was the first discoverer of the Trade wind, in 1492, was the first to discover this irregularity: and it is remarkable that it was of service to him in quieting the fears of his crew; who, having observed the constancy of the wind from the eastward, believed that they never would be able to get back to Spain. This irregular wind broke the spell, and much to the satisfaction of Columbus, who was then beginning to feel the inconvenience of that mutinous spirit which, in a later part of the voyage, had nearly cost him his life.—*Landfall of Columbus, by A. B. Becher, Captain, R.N., published by Potter, 31, Poultry, London.*

but only breezes of short duration. To the southward and westward of the Cape de Verd Islands the N.E. Trade blows more from the eastward.

In the vicinity of Trinidad, situated near the coast of Brazil, the S.E. Trade wind loses its prevailing direction, blowing more from the eastward, but frequent changes have been observed from S.E. to South, and also coming more generally from the northward than from the southward, as well as sudden gusts from the West. In this case and also in the foregoing the vicinity of the coasts of Africa and America doubtless occasion these disturbances.

It has been noticed that both the Trades are often more easterly in their direction, and blow with less strength during the night.

Variable Winds and Calms of the Torrid Zone.—The Trade winds are separated on their equatorial border by a zone of calms and changeable winds, varying considerably in extent from North to South. In this region calms, squalls, rain, and light breezes, blowing from all points of the horizon, are met with. During July and August this zone reaches further north of the equator, and is then found sometimes as far as the parallel of 12° and even of 13° North latitude. In December and January, on the contrary, it does not reach beyond 3° North latitude.

The following table is drawn up by Horsburgh, from observations extracted from the journals of two hundred and fifty ships, which have crossed the zone of the variable winds of the equator, between 30° and 40° West longitude.

Month.	Sailing South the N.E. Trade Wind is lost in North lat. from	Returning North the N.E. Trade Wind is found in North lat. from	Mean.	Returning North the S.E. Trade Wind is lost in latitude from	Sailing South the S.E. Trade Wind is found in North lat. from	Mean.	Lat. of the Zone of Variable Winds of the Torrid Zone.
	° °	° °	° ′	° °	° °	° ′	° ′
January..	5 to 10	3 to 6	5 45	0½ to 4 N.	2 to 4	2 45	3 0
February.	5 .. 10	2 .. 7	6 0	2 S... 3	0½.. 1	1 15	4 45
March ..	2½.. 8	2 .. 7	5 0	1 .. 2	0½.. 2½	1 15	3 45
April....	4 .. 9	4 .. 8	5 45	2 .. 2½	0 .. 2½	1 15	4 30
May	5 .. 10	4½.. 7	6 30	1 N... 4	0 .. 4	2 45	3 45
June	7 .. 13	7 .. 12	9 0	1 .. 5	0 .. 5	3 0	6 0
July	8½.. 15	11 .. 14	12 0	1 .. 6	1 .. 5	3 30	8 30
August ..	11 .. 15	11 .. 14½	13 0	3 .. 5	1 .. 3	3 15	9 45
Septemb.	9 .. 14	11 .. 14	14 45	2 .. 4	1 .. 3	3 0	8 45
October ..	7½.. 13	8½.. 14	10 0	2 .. 5	1 .. 5	3 0	7 0
Novemb..	6 .. 11	7 .. 10	8 0	3 .. 4	3 .. 5	3 45	4 15
Decemb ..	5 .. 7	3 .. 6	5 30	1 .. 4	1 .. 4½	3 55	2 30

Favourable Time for Crossing the Line.—The foregoing table shows the zone of the variable winds to be larger from June to December, and less from December to June—an important condition in making a voyage, because, as a ship crosses the equator from one hemisphere to the other, when passing from the North or South, the most favourable months for crossing the zone of the variables will be those from December to June. According to the time of crossing the passage will be several weeks longer or shorter, as it is more or less interrupted by calms, squalls, or variable winds near the equator. And we must also expect it to be the longest from these causes during the months of June, July, August, and September.

It may also be seen that, in the northern hemisphere, the N.E. Trade wind, according to the season, reaches more or less towards the equator, but rarely passes to the southward of it. On the contrary, the S.E. Trade wind reaches it easily, and extends northward of it sometimes even as far as 5° North latitude, in the neighbourhood of the coast of America.

Union of the Trades.—It happens, however, that the N.E. and S.E. Trade winds join each other generally somewhere about the meridian of 28° to 35° West, where a ship may pass perhaps in a squall from one of these winds to the other without experiencing any calm. Sometimes even in the vicinity of the African coast, and generally from December to February, the N.E. winds nearly join those from S.E. The different directions of the Trade winds from N.E. and S.E. occasion great uncertainty about the weather and the winds within their limits; an uncertainty which increases on approaching the zone of either. Besides this, it has been observed that near the equator the winds change more frequently from East to South than from East to North. We find occasionally in the region of the variables of the equator, and generally from July to September, winds which blow from West to N.W., and from West to South.

The preceding statements are of great importance in the general navigation of the Atlantic Ocean, and more particularly in that of the Gulf of Guinea. We shall apply them hereafter when alluding to the routes for crossing the Atlantic; for, according to that which may be adopted, the place of crossing the equator becomes important.

Extent of the Trade Winds.—The preceding observations on the winds of the first region of the Atlantic Ocean refer to a considerable distance from the coast, which has some effect in modifying their direction as well as their force. It is observed that the North and South Trade winds sometimes reach as far as the coasts of America, though they are not found regular till about 140 leagues from the African coast, and about 160 leagues from that part of it lying between Cape Palmas and Cape Verd. In this latitude, occasionally between June and September, and even till October, the variables are found even in 28° West longitude, blowing from West to N.W., and S.W., interrupted by calms, accompanied by rain and bad weather. The islands in this region also influence the Trade wind in their vicinity, but much less sensibly than the continent. The higher these islands are, the more frequent is rain about them, at least so observation has shown ; and it is generally found in the torrid zone that the wind which is constant at sea, becomes changeable near elevated and extensive coasts.

Force of the Trade Winds.—The S.E. Trade appears to have greater force than the N.E. Captain Maury, after many careful comparisons, estimated the force by the rate of sailing across the Trades as follows :—N.E. 5.6 per hour and the S.E. as nearly 8, but further comparisons carried on by Lieutenant de Brito, Portuguese R.N., very carefully corrected for various classes of ships, somewhat modify this estimate. He finds that in February and March the mean rate of crossing the N.E. Trade was 6.4. On the Eastern route (ships bound to Europe) the rate was only 6.2, whereas on the Western route (ships bound to the United States) the rate reached 6.7 miles per hour.

In August and September, on the same routes, the mean was only 5.7, the Eastern route being then the best, averaging 6.4, and the Western route only 4.8 miles per hour.

In February and March the rate of crossing the S.E. Trade on the Western route (outward bound vessels) was 7.0, and the Céntral route (homeward bound vessels) was 7.1. In August and September the Western route was 7.5 and the Central route 7.4.

These rates should be borne in mind, as during the intervening months it would appear that the strength of the N.E. Trade is to be found gradually progressing from the West in March, towards the East until September, when it returns to the westward.

Seasons of the Torrid Zone.—In the Atlantic Ocean, within the torrid zone, the weather is very variable, according to the latitude and time of year. It is observed that the atmosphere is more unsettled during the spring and autumn months, generally at the time of the equinoxes, than during the summer and winter months.

In this zone, North of the equator, the rainy season appears to vary in the following manner :—

From January to March it extends from the coast of Brazil as far as 20° W., the area of heavy rains not extending beyond 35° W.

From April to June the area of heavy rains is transferred to the African shore, extending to 20° W., but the whole region of the variables, almost to the coast of Brazil, is subject to tropical rain at this period.

From July to September the area of heavy rain extends from the African shore to 30° W., the rain-fall, however, extending as far as 45° W.

From October to December the area of heavy rain is, in mid-ocean, between 20° and 40° W., with more or less rain all round it.

As a general rule it may be assumed that in both hemispheres the rainy or winter season commences at any place when the sun, moving from the equator, passes the zenith of that place; and the dry season begins when the sun, returning towards the equator, has repassed the zenith of the same place.

Clearly as this law indicates the seasons, it is never-theless subject to many exceptions. Thus, the seasons do not begin and finish precisely at the period of these transits, but towards the time at which they take place. There is also always a period of uncertain weather, lasting a longer or shorter time, between each season, with variable winds, calms, and squalls, some of which have received the name of *tornadoes.*

In several places these squalls occur at the beginning and end of the rainy season, and limit the season of the great rains.

According to the foregoing law, it may be seen that the duration of the winter season at a place depends greatly on its latitude, and that it should be proportionably lengthened as it is nearer to the equator.

The hottest season within the torrid zone is that of winter, which is also the time of variables and calms. In the fine or dry season, on the contrary, the breezes are fresh and regular; this is generally the period when, near the coasts, land and sea breezes prevail with regularity.

At places within the immediate vicinity of the equator four seasons have been distinguished, two dry and two rainy; but, in reality, that part of the rainy season when rain is less abundant, and when rain squalls are separated by intervals of tolerable weather, has been considered one of the dry seasons.

Second Region of the Atlantic Ocean.—The second region of the Atlantic we have comprised between the parallel of 30° South and the South pole; in which two zones are distinguished, the frigid and temperate. Of the first:—

South Frigid Zone.—In the frigid zone, where but few navigators have penetrated, observations are necessarily few and these relate only to one season, namely, the summer; that being the only time when it can be penetrated to the South. The celebrated Cook, Admiral Dumont D'Urville, and Sir James Ross, are the principal navigators who have penetrated into this dreary region of the Atlantic; Cook proved that between 60° and 70° S. the winds are generally moderate; Foster adds that they often blow from the East. Cook has also observed that in those high latitudes the currents, though not strong, drift the ice towards the N.E., the North, and the N.W. D'Urville, after a stay of forty-nine days in that region, in which he could not penetrate beyond the latitude of 63° 33′ S., and was blocked up by the ice in 62° 22′ S. and 39° W., has left us the following observations, which appear in the voyage of the *Astrolabe* of 1837.

Variable winds from the East, between N.N.E., S.S.E., and South, for twenty-seven days; westerly winds varying from N.N.W. to S.S.W. twenty-two days, during the months of January, February, and the beginning of March. During this time the sloops *Astrolabe* and *Zelée* experienced a breeze from the North, accompanied by fog and rain, with winds from S.S.W. and S.W. the weather was alternately fine and cloudy; the winds from this quarter were in general moderate, and sometimes fresh.

The winds from N.E. and E.N.E., sometimes brought fine weather, but the sky was more frequently cloudy and foggy; snow fell principally with the winds from E.S.E. to N.N.W. by the N.E.; with the same breezes there was fog. Lastly, the strongest were those from East, E.S.E., and S.S.E., which in general blew very fresh.

Sir James Ross crossed the parallel of 60° S. latitude on the 23rd of December, 1842. During his stay in the frigid zone, which lasted till the 1st of March, he made observations on the winds, of which the following is a summary:—

December, 1842.—Winds from West changing from

N.W. to S.W., six days; winds from North, half a day; winds from South, a day and a half; winds from S.E., one day, moderate; those from South blowing very hard.

January, 1843.—Easterly winds changing from N.N.E. to S.E., twelve days; northerly winds, two days; southerly winds, three days and a half; westerly winds, varying from N.N.W. to S.S.W., thirteen days and a half. In this month, two days of strong breezes from N.W., the other winds fresh or moderate.

February.—Easterly winds changing from N.N.E. to S.S.E., eighteen days and a half; northerly winds, two days; South winds, three days; westerly winds, veering from N.W. to S.W., four days and a half. One day a hard gale from the North; one day, a stiff breeze from the East; the rest fresh or moderate.

From the preceding observations it appears that during the summer the frigid zone of the second region of the Atlantic Ocean, the East and West winds are tolerably equal, but that the East winds rather prevail.

Southern Temperate Zone.—In the temperate zone of this same region, westerly winds, extending as far as the tropic of Capricorn, and sometimes even to the latitude of 29° S., are predominant, varying from N.W. to S.W.; but the winds in this part of the Atlantic Ocean are changeable and irregular.

It has been remarked that in a zone comprised between the parallel of 28° and 35° S. latitude, the winds are extremely variable; but those most frequently met with are from N.E. to N.W.b.N. and from N.W. to S.W.b.W., principally during June, July, and August.

The prevailing westerly winds, varying from N.W. to S.W., between the parallels of 30° and 50° S., appear to be produced by the meeting of the returning currents from West to East, occasioned by the Trade winds (and named here tropical winds), with the polar currents proceeding from the poles towards the equator. The winds which result from these two currents of air ought to take almost a mean course, depending on the relative force of the two currents, and, consequently, this direction will be very variable, although it is generally from the West.

It has been observed that between 30° and 50° S. latitude, the winds blow periodically from S.W. to N.W.; thus, they vary from West to N.W. while the sun has South declination, and during the rest of the year they are in general from West to S.W., attended by bad weather. In this zone the easterly winds are never of long duration. When the winds shift to the South a calm soon takes place; and it has been observed that between Cape Horn and the Cape of Good Hope, when the wind continues from the North for several days in succession, it brings dark rainy weather; if these winds shift to South of West, the weather clears up and becomes fine.

Third Region of the Atlantic.—The third region of the Atlantic we comprise between the parallel of 30° N. latitude and the North pole, and is here divided, like the preceding one, into two zones—the frigid and temperate.

North Frigid Zone.—In the frigid zone, comprised between 60° N. latitude and the pole, and between Europe and America, and which includes Spitzbergen and Iceland, the winds are variable. The snow-clad lands in this zone, and the ice which prevails there, exercise a most powerful influence on the winds, varying them according to the seasons. The different navigators who have traversed this zone, in what is called the northern frozen ocean, have not observed any law in the winds, principally during summer. However, several of them agree in acknowledging that northerly winds are regular and prevalent.

Every wind in this zone is accompanied by a low temperature and snow, excepting in July and August, and a part of June. At this period, with southerly winds, the weather is tolerably fine, although attended by snow and rain. The same winds bring fog during those months. The coldest winds are those from North and N.E.; during June and July, winds from S.S.W. are frequently met with, sometimes blowing with much violence. In April and May, South winds are attended by snow; during the rest of the year there are thick fogs and very bad weather.

Spitzbergen.—At Spitzbergen it is said that during the first months of the year southerly winds prevail, and during the other months those from the North; but the S.E. and N.E. winds are those which bring most snow. Annexed are the observations of Sir

Edward Parry, during the months of May, June, July, and August, 1827, on the winds of those regions comprised between 70° and 82° 40′ N. latitude, as given in the narrative of his voyage towards the North pole in the *Hecla*.

North........	7½ days.	S.S.E.........	2 days.
N.N.W.......	5½ ,,	S.E...........	12 ,,
N.W.........	9 ,,	E.S.E.........	½ ,,
W.N.W.	2 ,,	East	17½ ,,
West........	13 ,,	E.N.E.	—
W.S.W.......	1 ,,	N.E.	9½ ,,
S.W.	9½ ,,	N.N.E.	11 ,,
S.S.W.	1 ,,	Calms	13½ ,,
South	4 ,,	Variables	4½ ,,

Nova Zembla.—At Nova Zembla, from September to May, northerly winds prevail almost without interruption; and from May till August those from West.

North Temperate Zone.—In the temperate zone, comprised between the latitudes 30° and 60° N., the prevailing winds, like those of the corresponding zone of the other hemisphere, are from the West, varying from N.W. to S.W. The prevailing West winds are doubtless produced by the same causes as those already stated in alluding to the corresponding zone of the southern hemisphere: by those currents of air named "tropical winds" blowing from West to East, and the polar currents directed from North to South. Their direction, therefore, depends on the relative intensity of these currents.

There is an important fact which shows the prevalence of S.W. winds in the temperate zone of the northern hemisphere, consisting in the difference of time occupied by the passage from the North of Europe to North America and that of the return passage home from North America to Europe. From Liverpool to New York the voyage is at least forty days; while from New York to Liverpool it is only about twenty.

The mean direction from whence is the prevailing wind of this zone, has been determined by Kramtz from numerous observations as follows: France S. 88° W.; England S. 66° W.; Germany S. 76° W.; Denmark S. 62° W.; Sweden S. 50° W.; Russia N. 87° W.; North America S. 86° W.; showing that Russia is the only country where the wind has a little North tendency in its source.

In the Atlantic Ocean the direction of the prevailing wind is generally from S. 45° W. to S. 70° W.

When the sun is in the northern hemisphere the prevailing westerly winds are S.W. and W.S.W.; if, on the contrary, the sun is in the southern hemisphere, they are from W.N.W. and N.W. The last period is that of gales and bad weather between North America and Europe.

CHAPTER II.

Land and Sea Breezes of the Tropics—The General Theory concerning them—The Harmattan and its Peculiarities — Tornadoes, their Seasons and Range—Winds off the Cape of Good Hope.

Having described the winds met with *at sea* in the Atlantic Ocean, it remains for us now, in order to complete our view of the winds of this ocean, to allude to those experienced on its coasts. We shall commence with the coast of Africa, offering first some general remarks as to that coast.

Land and Sea Breezes.—Land and Sea breezes blow on certain parts of the Atlantic coast with great regularity, particularly on those between the tropics and among the islands situated in the torrid zone, so much so that they might be reckoned among the periodical winds. In general the sea breeze blows during the day, and the land breeze commencing towards evening lasts part of the night, blowing in the opposite direction; it commonly ceases shortly after sunrise, and rarely lasts beyond nine or ten o'clock in the morning. They afford valuable assistance to the navigator, enabling him to find a fair wind where it is generally foul, by placing his ship at a moderate distance from the land, so as to be within their influence. Philosophers attribute these winds to the difference of temperature between the sea and the land.

It is observed that in the neighbourhood of the coast of Morocco, the sea breeze comes most frequently from N.W.; on the coast of Guinea from South to S.W.; and on that of Loango and Congo from S.W. to West. These breezes generally blow alternately with those from the land. They are generally found as stated near the coast, but they sometimes prevail far from it, gradually losing their force, until they are opposed and overcome by the general winds. The parts where these changes occur are almost always subject to storms, accompanied by rain or calm.

The following general view is given by philosophers of the causes producing alternate land and sea breezes. In the morning, the temperature of the land and sea being nearly alike, the air is at rest. But when the sun rises above the horizon and the earth becomes more heated than the water, the sea breeze begins gradually to take its place, the heated air ascending, and that from the sea coming to replace it: gentle at first, but gradually gaining force, till it attains its height with the greatest heat of the day. It then diminishes gradually with the decrease of temperature till night; when an interval of calm takes place. Again, during the night, when the land is colder than the sea, the land breeze rises, and attains its greatest strength at the time of the lowest temperature of the night. It continues until day, still becoming weaker, and sometimes even until eight or nine o'clock in the morning, according to the latitude. A knowledge of these phenomena is highly useful, and is particularly advantageous in local navigation, where it may be turned to good account in shortening passages.

Solar Breezes.—There are yet, on some parts of the western coast of Africa, certain winds, which may be called solar, their changes appearing to be regulated by the influence of the sun. We find them principally in the North, on the coast of Senegambia; and also on that extending from Cape Lopez to Cape Negro, south of the equator.

On the former coast these winds vary from N.E. to N.W.; on the latter from S.E. and South to S.W. and even to W.S.W. The course of these winds, which blow strong on the coast of Senegambia, principally from November till April; and on the other from October till March, and even April, is as follows:—The breeze at sea lasts through the day, strengthening in the afternoon, and weakening towards the evening; during the night it changes, and blows more along the land.

In navigating these two coasts, a ship should regulate her sailing so as to be near the land when the night breeze springs up, and out at sea when that of the day begins. But in navigating the whole coast of Africa, north of the Bights, a haze varying in density will be found from the vicinity of the land to forty or fifty leagues out to sea. It is very well known to consist of the finer particles of sand. And it is so thick as to cover the weather side of the rigging, giving it a dirty, slovenly appearance. It is in this fine sand that minute insects (*infusoriæ*), that are known to belong to South America, have been found by naturalists. These winds, the variations of which belong to the alternate land and sea breezes, do not, however, blow directly from the shore. They are sometimes very strong, even at a short distance from the coast; and in order to profit by them short boards need only be made of twelve, fifteen, or thirty miles at farthest from it.

The Harmattan.—The harmattan is a wind peculiar to the western coast of Africa; it blows from East, changing to E.N.E. on the North coast, from the parallel of Madeira to that of the River Gaboon, following what are called the latter rains. But on this coast it sets in about a month earlier than near the Gambia: setting in at any time of the day or night, and lasting from a day to a week or even a fortnight. The period of the moon is no rule for its recurrence—it is generally a moderate breeze, not so violent as the sea breeze, but still sufficiently so to produce a change in the direction of the current which sets along the coast. It is sometimes very strong on the coasts of Senegal and Senegambia, but often light on the coast of Guinea. It is a cold, dry wind, generally lasting for a series of three, six, or nine days, principally between the end of November and February or March. It reaches, however, but a short distance from the coast, about three or four leagues beyond which it is no longer found, but the effects of it on the temperature are experienced at thirty or forty miles from it. It sometimes commences at sunrise and ends in the afternoon. This wind is always accompanied by fog, and sometimes loaded with a fine reddish dust, so thickly, that nothing can be distinguished, particularly near the coast, at a trifling distance.

The harmattan is an extraordinary dry wind, and produces the most singular effects. It dries up every particle of moisture in the atmosphere, parching the skin, drying the planks of the sides and deck so as to render the seams leaky; and loosening casks by drying the staves so that the hoops fall off, unless they are attended to. In fact, its effects in evaporation may be estimated by the circumstances that while the annual amount of this on the coast is 64 inches, the effect of the harmattan raises it to 134 inches. The hazy atmosphere which is peculiar to the African coast within the limits above-mentioned, is always increased during the harmattan, and assists in the deceptive appearance of the shore, making it appear much *further* off than it really is. Great caution should be exercised in making allowance for this. It is said to be generally healthy, though certainly very disagreeable and inconvenient. The greatest advantage derived from it, nevertheless, is the production of gum. It suddenly arrests in trees the circulation of sap that is flowing rapidly at the season when the winter rains are just ended, and causes it to exude from the wood, thus forming the gum which constitutes the principal commercial greatness of Senegal.

Tornadoes.—Tornadoes, which generally mark the commencement and end of the rainy season, are violent squalls of about three hours' duration, well known on the West coast of Northern Africa. In the South they are seldom felt, and if so are always slight. The name is derived from the sudden changing or veering of the wind while they last. Their approach is made known long beforehand by clouds of a dull yellow colour, which by night are very black. They originate in the North and N.E., and generally move against the prevailing wind. Tornadoes are generally distinguished by electric phenomena, and they gradually overcome the prevailing wind.

Every precaution becomes necessary to meet a tornado. Its prognostics are, dark heavy clouds gradually spreading on the horizon, and lifting slowly, leaving an extensive arch clear and distinct, furrowed every now and then by lightning; the clearer the arch is defined the more violent will be the approaching storm.

A few moments of calm then ensue, and the N.E. wind is suddenly felt coming violently and rapidly with the storm, which breaks forth in all its fury when the arch attains the height of thirty or forty degrees above the horizon.

From N.E. the wind veers rapidly to East or S.E. blowing with the same force. The storm afterwards ceases with rain; when the wind slackens in force it veers to the South, and when it becomes still less to

S.W. A calm frequently succeeds a tornado ; and it is found that when the wind precedes the rain, the storm is more violent.

Vessels to meet these passing squalls, which rarely last more than an hour and a half, should shorten all sail, and furl if possible. We never know what the extent of them may be. Sometimes they have the force of hurricanes of short duration, in which the wind changes so suddenly that a sail might be split and inevitably lost.

The S.W. winds of the West coast of Africa are often disturbed at certain periods (especially in the winter), for we find in the Mediterranean, and on the coast of Portugal, intense polar currents, which, increasing the rapidity of the Trade wind from North, forces it abruptly toward the equator. The meeting of these winds and those from S.W., prevailing at this period, contributes, perhaps, to produce tornadoes. They are very frequent in the Northern hemisphere, and also very violent. South of the equator, on the contrary, as already observed, these disturbances of the atmosphere are rarely found.

On the coast of Gaboon, and in the Gulf of Biafra, tornadoes blowing from N.W. to West and S.W. sometimes, though very rarely, occur. In the northern hemisphere their visits are mostly at the commencement of the winter season, and consequently the time of their appearance varies according to the place. Thus, they are found at Cape Palmas a month earlier than at Sierra Leone; while at Goree and St. Louis, to the northward, they are a month and a half after they have prevailed at Sierra Leone. They visit several localities exactly at the end of the winter season, those principally from the archipelago of the Bissagos to Cape Palmas and the coast of Guinea. In the Gulf of Guinea they come chiefly in the months of March, April, and May, and they again occur at some places during November and December.

South of the equator tornadoes blow chiefly from S.E., and take place from March to June, as well as from September to October. They diminish in force in proportion as they are found to the South; and in the latitude of the Congo it is not unusual for storms, without much wind, to form in the East, and passing South, to terminate in the S.W. They are much like the storms which are encountered in the northern hemisphere. These are somewhat similar to tornadoes in the changes of the wind, but not in force.

On the coasts of Angola and Benguela, towards the evenings of November and December, storms of this description are found, but very rarely accompanied by much wind. On the contrary, the clouds heap together, and the wind falls gradually to a calm. These clouds generally become scattered at ten or eleven o'clock at night, and at the same time a feeble land breeze rises, which usually lasts during the remainder of it.

Cape of Good Hope.—About two hundred leagues West of the Cape of Good Hope, S.E. winds prevail from October to March, and even April. In the same latitude, from May to August, at a hundred leagues to the West of the Cape, winds changing mostly from N.W. to S.W., are found, bringing a high sea with dirty weather. The same winds extend two hundred leagues to the East of the Cape of Good Hope, and the weather becomes worse as it is approached, during this season, from East to West.

N.W. winds here bring fog, rain, and haze; but when they blow from S.W. the weather is fine and cold. During April and May these winds are found equally to the East and West of the Cape, but only as sudden gusts. These gusts are preceded by black clouds gathering in the West. The wind then begins blowing violently from W.N.W. to West, and then changes rapidly to S.W.; it then passes to the South, afterwards moderates, and soon after a calm ensues.

Doubling the Cape of Good Hope from Eastward.—When the season is advanced, D'Apres de Mannivilette advises a ship that would round the Cape from the East, not to go further than forty miles from land, and not nearer to it than eighteen miles, in order to preserve a latitude where the winds are less violent and the sea not so high as to the southward.

These stormy winds are very frequent during the winter. They are accompanied by so much rain, that sometimes two successive fine days can scarcely be found. According to several authorities, this bad weather is felt as far East as Madagascar.

On the parallel of 36° S. latitude, at 200 or 250

leagues from the Cape of Good Hope, to the East and West of the Cape, the N.W. winds, which are so violent near it, become moderate, and frequently vary to S.S.W. Generally between the parallels of 33° and 36° S. latitude, the West winds appear to prevail.

When doubling the Cape from the eastward, on the approach of a South-easter it is recommended to keep just off the bank of Agulhas, where smoother water may then be probably found than on it; and where the N.W. current then runs strongest. A vessel experiencing tedious westerly gales forty miles off the land, may frequently find fine weather by standing in upon the coast, for they often remit in violence near the land several days previous to their terminating outside.

But when on rounding the Cape from the eastward, both in winter and in summer, with an approaching gale from N.W., West, or S.W., it is better to stand in for the bank, making short boards if possible till the gale is over, keeping in 75 to 55 fathoms water. The gale will blow itself out at S.W., following the course of the sun.

A South-wester off the Cape is indicated by an unnaturally clear sky, a well-defined horizon, a falling barometer, and thunder and lightning.

A South-easter off the Cape is indicated by the same remarkably clear sky, with light scud flying, and a steadily rising barometer. The lighter it commences the more wind may be expected, and from that and the long swell the heavy nature of the gale may be anticipated.

Doubling the Cape from Westward.—Consequently, when doubling the Cape from the West, it will be best to keep well off the land South of the parallel of lat. 35° S., and to enter the Indian Ocean between that and 40°. In adopting this course, a vessel would also profit by the *cross* current of the Atlantic Ocean setting eastward.

Winds at the Cape of Good Hope.—At the Cape of Good Hope and in Table Bay the months of September, October, and November form the spring; those of December, January, and February, the summer; March, April, and May are the autumn; and June, July, and August, the winter months. The following table, constructed from observations made in the course of many years at Cape Town, shows the prevalent winds during the year and in each month.

Months.	Winds.	Remarks.
January ..	S.E.	Dry, hot, occasional rain, with wind from N.W.
February ..	S.E.	Temperature variable, heavy rain occasionally with N.W. winds.
March	S.E.	Heavy gusts from N.W.; thunder; light rain and mist.
April	S.E. & N.W.	Heavy gusts; temperature variable, and mist.
May	N.W.	Fine at the beginning of the month; thunder and tempestuous at the end.
June	N.W.	Heavy gusts sometimes from S.E. or N.E.; rain, thunder, and stormy.
July	N. & N.N.W.	Frequent gusts of wind; cold, mist, snow, rain, hail.
August	N.W.	Ditto.
September.	S.E.	Weather changeable and mild.
October ..	N.W.	Heavy rain; thunder and lightning.
November..	N.W. & S.E.	Hot dry weather; moderate breezes.
December..	S.E.	When the wind blows from N.W. the breezes are light—the weather hot and dry.

The summer at the Cape is from October to April, in which season ships are considered safe in Table Bay.

N.W. gales are experienced there in every season of the year, but they seldom blow home in Table Bay from November to May. The Dutch fixed the 10th of May for all ships to leave it, N.W. winds being then expected, when a mountainous sea is thrown into the bay and the anchorage is dangerous.

The prevailing winds near the Cape are from the S.E. and South in summer; S.E. winds blow frequently in every month of the year, but generally bring settled weather. N.E. winds are less frequent than any, and never durable. In May, June, July, and August, the West and S.W. winds blow strong, attended with foggy cloudy weather; but the N.W. winds are most violent in these months, lasting for several days, and sometimes accompanied with lightning, hail showers, or rain.

When the Table Mountain, in summer, begins to be covered with a white cloud, a strong S.E. or E.S.E. wind is coming. In January, February, and March, these winds are strong on the Table and Devil Mountains, and drive through the gap between them white clouds like woolly fleeces over the perpendicular sides of the Table Mountain. Vessels not well moored are then liable to drive and bring both anchors ahead, and even with all anchors down, sometimes not regaining the anchorage for five or six days. When the Table Mountain is free from clouds, the South-easter will be moderate, and a gentle sea breeze then generally blows in on the western side of the bay, while a fresh S.E. wind prevails on the eastern side of it half-way across during most of the day.

Table Mountain, like a huge wall, receives some four miles in breadth of the current, which bounds up with diminishing temperature, and deposits the celebrated table cloth or cap on the top.

The upper surface of this white cap is smoothed off like a well dressed peruke; its North border hangs over the precipice, drapery fashion, but, during a very strong wind it pours down like a cataract to about 1,000 feet from the top, where, entering a warmer temperature, it dissolves and disappears.

The black South-easter cap differs from the preceding by the nimbus tint of a canopy of cloud which projects on the southern side of the mountain, and from which light rain occasionally falls.

The strong southerly winds are indicated by the tops of the higher elevations on each side of False Bay becoming covered in rapid succession from the South; but they seldom remain covered throughout the gale.

The temperature of the winter months,—June, July, and August,—is 55°. The prevailing winds are from the N.N.W., West, and occasionally S.W., and they are generally accompanied by rain. Hail-storm squalls are usually from the S.W. As seen from the Observatory, the first indicator of a North-wester is the appearance of a mass of condensed vapour rolling over the Lions' Hill and enveloping the signal station; also the air feels damp and a swell sets into Table Bay; the tops of the ridges bordering the shore in the direction of Hout Bay become covered, and next, but not always, Table Mountain.

Strong winds with squalls and showers, more or less heavy, follow these harbingers, and the fogs which now cover the elevations are of the usual European cast. The phenomena which are characteristic of warm dry air being forced upwards by strong wind, and again descending, are here entirely wanting.

The duration of a North-wester is from two days to a week, and sometimes ten days.

Low fogs occasionally occur in the winter and autumn, namely, the fogs of calm weather, above which the tops of mountains, high hills, and topmasts of ships are visible, and which are dispersed by the heat of the sun.

In the fair weather season, regular sea breezes from S.W. and West prevail in the morning, and continue till noon or longer. These are followed by strong S.E. winds from the land, which blow fresh during the afternoon, and frequently till the following morning; then the sea breeze returns.

Previous to the construction of the breakwater and docks, vessels could not remain in Table Bay during the winter season after the beginning of May, the N.W. gales being so violent, but the completion of these works renders it a commodious place for vessels to refit when necessary. The approach of winter in the neighbourhood of the Cape of Good Hope is indicated by the prevailing S.E. winds being interrupted occasionally, and also lessening in force.

We conclude this chapter with the symbolic method of Admiral Sir Francis Beaufort for expressing the force of the wind, and the state of the weather; the former by numbers and the latter by letters. This method has been adopted by the Admiralty for the use of the Royal Navy, on account of the evident advantage of the space which it leaves in a log for recording the general proceedings of the ship, besides preserving a more faithful register with it of the weather than by the old mode of describing it. The figures may be considered as applied to the annexed table, showing the strength and velocity of the wind. The advantage of using twelve gradations of force will be seen as affording range for the judgment, free from considerable error, and allows for the virtue which some ships possess of carrying more sail than others without being distressed by it, from their superior stability. The amount of pressure in pounds on the square foot for each of these gradations of strength, as well as the space travelled over by the wind are added in the table which follows, forming an interesting subject for reference.

FIGURES.

To denote the force of the Winds.

0—Calm		
1—Light Air	Just sufficient to give	Steerage way
2—Light Breeze....	with which a well-conditioned man-of-war, under all sail, and clean full, would go in smooth water, from	1 to 2 knots
3—Gentle Breeze ..		3 to 4 knots
4—Moderate Breeze.		5 to 6 knots
5—Fresh Breeze....	in which the same ship could just carry closed hauled......	Royals, &c.
6—Strong Breeze ..		Single-reefs and top-gallant sails
7—Moderate Gale ..		Double-reefs, jib, &c.
8—Fresh Gale......		Triple-reefs, courses, &c.
9—Strong Gale		Close-reefs & courses
10—Whole Gale	with which she could only bear	Close-reefed main topsail and reefed foresail
11—Storm	with which she would be reduced to......	Storm stay sails
12—Hurricane	to which she could show	No canvas

B.F.	Pressure in lbs. on Square Foot.	Feet travelled per Second.	Miles travelled per Hour.
1	0·003	1·2	0·84
2	0·031	3·8	2·55
3	0·135	8·1	5·34
4	0·460	14·7	9·87
5	0·981	21·4	14·48
6	1·381	25·7	17·5
7	1·661	28·2	19·2
8	2·342	33·2	22·7
9	4·166	44·5	30·3
10	10·400	70·3	47·7
11	26·033	111·4	75·9
12	52·033	157·4	105·8
	62·400	173·1	120·0*

* Utmost observed.

Letters.

To denote the State of the Weather.

b—Blue Sky—whether with clear or hazy atmosphere.

c—Cloudy—*i.e.*, Detached opening clouds.

d—Drizzling rain.

f—Fog—f Thick Fog.

g—Gloomy Dark Weather.

h—Hail.

l—Lightning.

m—Misty or Hazy—so as to interrupt the view.

o—Overcast—*i.e.* The whole sky covered with one impervious cloud.

p—Passing Showers.

q—Squally.

r—Rain—*i.e.* Continuous rain.

s—Snow.

t—Thunder.

u—Ugly threatening appearance of the Weather.

v—Visibility of Distant Objects—whether the sky be cloudy or not.

w—Wet Dew.

.—Under any letter denotes an Extraordinary Degree.

By the combination of these letters all the ordinary phenomena of the weather may be recorded with certainty and brevity.

EXAMPLES.

bcm—Blue Sky, with detached opening clouds, but hazy round the horizon.

gv—Gloomy dark weather, but distant objects *remarkably* visible.

qpdlt—Very hard squalls, and showers of drizzle, accompanied by lightning, with very heavy thunder.

CHAPTER III.

African Coast from the Cape to the Straits of Gibraltar—Winds at the Cape—Benguela and Angola—Congo—The Bights—Fernando Po—The Windward and Gold Coast—Sierra Leone—Cape Verds—Canaries—Madeira.

Winds of the West Coast of Africa between the Cape of Good Hope and Cape Palmas.—If a line be drawn from the Cape of Good Hope to Cape Palmas, it will nearly be that of separation between the S.E. Trade winds and those prevailing winds, varying from S.S.E. to S.S.W. and S.W., which blow during the whole year in that part of the ocean between the above line and the West coast of Africa. The distance from the coast at which these winds prevail is variable, and they are found much stronger on approaching the Cape. It has also been remarked that on this part of the African coast the wind frequently takes a direction making an angle of about two points with the line of the coast.

At eighty or a hundred leagues from the North coast of Guinea, and on the line of separation above mentioned, the Trade wind is generally found; which at this distance begins also to incline towards the coast, and in proportion as it is nearer to it draws to South and S.S.W. and even to S.W. On this limit of the Trade wind, calms, storms, and variable winds are generally found.

Hottentot Coast.—From October to March land and sea breezes are regular as far as the tropic, beyond which steady S.S.W. winds prevail, increasing in strength to the southward. No rain falls, but there are heavy night dews.

The S.S.W. wind lasts until May, when northerly winds are frequent until August—heavy rollers set in after these winds. The prevailing S.S.W. wind then returns.

The wind frequently veers from S.S.E. to S.S.W. with heavy gusts. In proportion as the coast is left, these breezes diminish in strength, veering to South and S.S.E., and gradually joining the S.E. Trade.

Near the coast fogs and haze are very prevalent during the forenoon.

Gales may be expected at the full and change of the moon.

Coasts of Benguela and Angola.—On the coast of Benguela and Angola the weather is generally fine all the year except during the months of March and April. In November, December, January, and February, S.S.W. winds blow fresh: also S.W. and W.S.W., and now and then those from W.N.W.; so that in these months navigation is easy on this coast. In November and December there is sometimes a little small rain, especially in the mornings, with the wind from S.E. or at least South. Directly it draws to S.W. the weather clears off, and the sky suddenly lightens up. Sometimes, again, there are appearances of stormy weather and lightning, particularly in the evenings: but, as already noticed, these storms bring but little wind, and this frequently falls away until it gradually becomes calm. These appearances seldom, as already stated, last longer than ten or eleven o'clock at night; and then a gentle land breeze rises, which generally lasts till morning. March and April are the two worst months of the year, on account of their stormy character. However, as soon as the wind veers to S.W. the sky clears and the weather becomes fine. The land breeze then comes on from S.E., and sometimes from N.E.; but these gusts are quite unlike the tornadoes North of the equator.

During the "fine season," from May to October, the sky is often overcast, especially in the morning, and the sea breeze is then seldom strong: while, on the contrary, it rarely fails when the sky becomes clear, and is still fresher when it clears quickly. In May and June the calms are less. The sea breeze begins late, and the land wind is fresh till after sunrise. In July, August, September, and October, S.W. winds are fresh and well established. They are found near the coast at ten or eleven o'clock in the morning; falling towards sunset, they rarely continue later than seven or eight o'clock in the evening. During October they sometimes last till midnight, and are followed by

http://www.amazon.ca

SDw3JLB3LR

Billing Address/Adresse de correspondance:
Dorit Girash
18 Bayshore Dr
Leamington, ON N8H 4A8
Canada

Shipping Address/Adresse d'expédition:
Dorit Girash
18 Bayshore Dr
Leamington, ON N8H 4A8
Canada

Invoice for/Bon de livraison pour

Your order of/Votre commande du:April 26, 2013
Order ID/N° commande: 702-7282241-5449029

Invoice number/N° bon de livraison Dw3JLB3LR May 13, 2013

Quantity/Quantité	Item/Article	Description/Description	Our Price/Notre prix	Total/Total
1	Navigation of the Atlantic Ocean; With an Account of the Winds, Weather and Currents Found Therein ... Fourth and Enlarg... **(** P-1-A166E876 **)** **1241091161**	Paperback	CDN$ 23.13	CDN$ 23.13

Subtotal/Sous-total	CDN$ 23.13
Shipping and Handling/Frais de port	CDN$ 2.48
GST/HST/TPS/TVH	CDN$ 1.28
PST/RST/QST/TVP/TVD/TVQ	CDN$ 0.00
Order Total/Montant total	CDN$ 26.89
Paid via/Payé par Mastercard	CDN$ 26.89
Balance Due/Montant dû	CDN$ 0.00

This shipment completes your order.

You can always check the status of your orders from the "Your Account" link on our home page.

Thanks for shopping at Amazon.ca, and please come again!

Cette livraison complète votre commande.

Vous pouvez à tout moment consulter l'état de votre commande grâce au lien "Votre compte" sur notre page d'accueil.

Merci de faire confiance à Amazon.ca Revenez nous voir!

Amazon.com.ca,Inc. 410 Terry Avenue North Seattle, WA 98109-5210
GST Registration Number/N° enregistrement TPS 85730 5932 RT0001 / QST Registration Number/ N° enregistrement TVQ 1201187016 TQ0001 / RST Registration Number/N° enregistrement TVD 85730 5932 MT0001 / PST Registration Number/N° enregistrement TVP PST-1017-2103

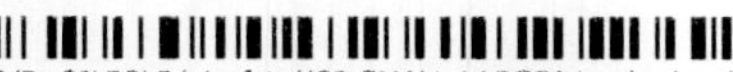

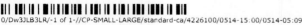

0/Dw3JLB3LR/-1 of 1-//CP-SMALL-LARGE/standard-ca/4226100/0514-15:00/0514-05:09

JM8

the land breeze till eight or nine o'clock in the morning. In the interval between these breezes there is sometimes a calm.

Coast of Congo.—On the coast of Congo the winds are generally moderate, and from September to March between South and West. From March to October the prevailing winds are from S.S.E., and are sometimes strong from between East and North. Strong sea breezes are sometimes found between North and West, generally from April to August. During this season there are very heavy rains. In the fine season, from September to March, the land and sea breezes succeed each other regularly. But they are not so regular during the rainy season, which lasts only three months, from November till February.

River Congo.—In the River Congo the seasons and winds are nearly the same as on the coast to the South of this river; observing, that the further South the later are the seasons. Thus, in the River Congo the rainy season is from October to January.

Coast of Loango.—On the coast of Loango, from September to March, the prevailing winds are from South to West. In December and January strong winds prevail from West and S.W. From March to October the wind is generally from S.S.E., changing to South and S.S.W.

The alternate land and sea breezes are very regular on this coast, except during the rainy season—from September to December. Tornadoes take place in March, April, May, and often in September and

October; sometimes also in January and February. These tornadoes, generally less violent than those North of the equator, are, however, sufficiently severe to render it necessary for ships to reduce all sail.

Cape Lopez.—Off Cape Lopez, from June to October the wind is generally from South, moderate, as well as that from S.S.W., which wind prevails during the other months. In the first half of the year fine weather prevails, with light southerly winds. From Benguela to Cape Lopez the wind in shore becomes more westerly, but draws more southerly as the distance from the shore is increased.

At the end of November storms with heavy rains occur. The tornadoes are most severe in March and April. They also occur in November, December, and January; as well as storms which differ from tornadoes only by the wind being less violent.

Gulf of Biafra.—On the eastern shore of the Gulf of Biafra, two seasons only are generally known; that of tornadoes and bad weather lasting from March till the middle of September. July and August are comparatively the dry months, in which the S.S.W. breezes are fresh; they veer to S.E. sometimes and blow fresh, commencing North of the equator as far as lat. 2° or 3°. The rainy season begins in September and lasts till March. This is the time of calms and light breezes from South to W.S.W.

The islands of the Gulf of Biafra—Princes Island, St. Thomas, and Anno Bom—have the same winds as the adjacent coast. The alternate land and sea breezes are more regular and fresh near them, and cease about the time of the rainy season. The former never reach far from the coast either of the continent or the island.

Coasts of Biafra, Benin, and St. Paul to Cape Palmas.—On the North coast of the Gulf of Biafra and Benin, and on the shore of the Gulf of Guinea, a moderate wind from S.W. to West prevails, with more or less regularity, according to the season, during the whole year. The harmattan on this coast blows in November, December, and January, from the East, but never strong.

From October to February, the period called the fine season, alternate land and sea breezes are found near the coast. The former never extend further than four leagues off shore and are always weak. The tornadoes on this coast occur from March to June. In April and May, in the Gulf of Benin and Biafra, one may be looked for every forty-eight hours, and frequently two in one day, and extremely violent, they occasionally occur in October and November. On the Ivory and Gold coasts they last till June. The period of heavy rains in the Gulf of Benin and Biafra is from August to September, but on the Ivory and Gold coasts it is from May to June.

The fogs (commonly known as the "smokes,") which are very thick upon this part of the coast of Africa, take place in July, August, and September on the Ivory and Gold coasts, also from December to February. In the Gulfs of Benin and Biafra, they are particularly found from October to May. These fogs generally commence at three o'clock in the morning, and clear away towards ten or eleven in the forenoon.

It may be observed here that this part of the African coast has received the name of the "Windward Coast," including all that between Cape Mount and the Assinee River, at which the Gold coast begins, and is again sub-divided into the Grain or Pepper coast, the Ivory coast, and the Adou or Quaqua coast. Again, the Gold coast extends from the Assinee to the Volta. The weather on the Windward coast is fine the first five months of the year, with light southerly winds: but in May S.E. winds become strong, thunder and lightning are frequent, and rain occasionally, which, with the great rains, last till September. The weather again becomes fine to the end of the year.

Island of Fernando Po.—In the island of Fernando Po the climate is the same as that of the Gulf of Biafra adjacent to it. The harmattan blows there from December to February,—the most healthy season of the year. On the coasts above mentioned, and at Fernando Po, in the rainy season the alternate land and sea breezes either fail or blow irregularly.

At the island of *St. Helena*, S.E. winds blow during nearly the whole year. They are only interrupted for a few days during this interval by light westerly winds, principally in June, July, and November; in which last month there are generally a few days of westerly wind.

Ascension Island.—At the island of Ascension the winds are the same as at St. Helena, continuing moderate during the whole year.

On the African coast included between Cape Mesurado and Cape Verd the researches of Major Rennell have led him to the conclusion that as the sun gets into the northern hemisphere a total change takes place in the winds of this part. Instead of N.E. and S.E. winds they become N.W. and S.W., extending over to the western borders of the Atlantic in 40° W., between about 8° and 15° N., producing an easterly current within those limits that joins the Guinea current. Again, Maury also says these winds are mostly found from July to October inclusive, when the sun is again coming South.

On this part of the coast in the months of June, July, and August, the S.W. winds are occasionally very strong, with abundance of rain. But they do not last more than a few hours, then falling calm, and leaving a short troublesome sea. As the sun draws to the South, these S.W. winds are less frequent, they draw to the South and S.E., becoming light. A tolerably certain indication of wind is lightning, for it seldom fails to come from the quarter in which that is seen. When the moon is at the full or change, squally unsettled weather may generally be expected. At these times the S.W. winds are most severe, but especially in July. They come in heavy squalls with abundance of rain, and produce N.E. currents. On the part of the coast in question, indeed the whole coast between 20° N. and the equator, the rainy season is from July to October inclusive, the sun passing the zenith of all those places on its way to the southward.

Cape Palmas and Liberia.—In the latitude of Cape Palmas, and to the South of this cape, the prevailing wind is W.S.W. To the North of the Cape, it is from S.W. and S.S.W., and during the fine season (from December to March) it varies from W.S.W. to W.N.W. The rainy season here lasts from May to October. The same winds prevail on the coast of Liberia.

The great rains fall principally in July and August. In April and May there are violent tornadoes, but they cease during the heavy rains and recommence in October and November. During the fine season the alternate land and sea breezes are very regular: the former are found twelve miles from the coast. The land breeze varies from N.N.W. to N.N.E., and lasts from noon to midnight. The sea breeze varies from W.S.W. to W.N.W., changing very gradually, and at the middle of the season becomes North. It changes to South at the end and beginning of the season, and shifts, according to circumstances, eastward or westward. There is often an interval of calm between the land and sea breezes. But in the rainy season on this coast it is observed that the land wind seldom blows: the winds from S.W. bringing with them much swell. The harmattan blows in December, but only occasionally, and then is not strong. It is neither so cold nor so disagreeable as on the coast to the North of Cape St. Anne.

It has been observed that on the coast of Liberia, during the rainy season, the weather is not so bad on shore as it is thirty or forty miles out at sea. Thus, in this season, at that distance, calms, rains, and baffling winds are found, and even storms and tornadoes; in both of which the wind is mostly from East, but not strong.

Coast of Sierra Leone.—On the coast of Sierra Leone, during the fine season—from November to April—the prevailing wind is from N.N.W. to N.W. In the winter season it is S.W., changing to W.S.W. and W.N.W., blowing sometimes strong from West. The harmattan is sometimes severe in November and December; then, during the following months, it becomes moderate. It is not permanent, and blows only at intervals, varying between E.S.E. and N.E.

Tornadoes occur in May. During the great rains from June to September, they partly cease, and return in September, October, and November. In the winter season the sea breeze is generally light, changing from S.W. to W.S.W. and interrupted by N.W. winds.

During the fine season, from the Isles de Los to Cape St. Anne, alternate land and sea breezes prevail, from W.S.W. and E.N.E., *passing by the North.* The sea breeze lasts from ten or eleven o'clock in the morning till midnight. The change in the land and sea breezes takes place round by the north, after an interval of calm or only a successive change of wind from W.N.W. and N.W. to North and N.E.

In taking a general view of this coast, the prevailing winds are found to be from the westward; from W.N.W. during the fine season; and from W.S.W. and S.W. during the rainy season, or from May to November.

The following table of wind and weather has been compiled from numerous observations at Sierra Leone during the year. The numbers in the columns express days.

Months.	Winds.	Fine.	Cloud.	Mist or Fog.	Rain.	Remarks.
Jan. ..	N.W.	31	..	..	..	Sea breeze p.m.; harmattan a.m.
Feb. ..	N.W.	28	..	..	..	Storms with rain.
March	N.W.	30	1	..	..	Tornadoes.
April..	N.W. to S.W.	26	..	4	..	Ditto.
May ..	S.E. to S.W.	14	..	5	12	Tornadoes cease; partial storms.
June..	S.E. to S.W.	14	..	3	13	Rain with S.E. winds; intense heat.
July ..	S.E. & S.W.	5	..	3	23	Ditto.
Aug. ..	S.E. & S.W.	2	..	..	29	Ditto.
Sept...	E. & S.W.	10	..	..	20	Tornadoes.
Oct. ..	W.N.W. & S.W.	20	..	5	6	Cloudy; oppressive heat.
Nov...	N.E & W.N.W.	21	..	4	5	Ditto.
Dec. ..	N.E. & N.W.	23	..	4	4	Do.; thnd. and lghtn. towards even.

Coast and Archipelago of Bissagos.—On the coast and archipelago of Bissagos, the West winds, changing from W.N.W. to S.W., prevail during nine months of the year. They blow in the winter season (from May to October) without interruption from W.N.W. to S.W.b.W., and sometimes with violence during July and August. Tornadoes take place principally in June, and also in September and October.

The harmattan blows (and sometimes with much strength) in November, December, January, and the beginning of February. In the fine season, along the coast and in the archipelago, alternate land and sea breezes are found. Those from the land blow from N.E. to E.N.E. and E.S.E. till eight or nine in the morning, then till eleven or twelve o'clock there is calm, which is succeeded by the sea breeze, rising from W.N.W. or W.S.W. It lasts till past sunset, and is succeeded by the land breeze, which rises towards midnight.

Coast of Senegambia.—On the coast of Senegambia, during the fine season (from September or October until May), the prevailing winds are N.E., changing to N.W. by the North. The solar breezes are settled and regular on this coast; they are mostly moderate, though occasionally strong.

The harmattan blows with violence in November, December, and January; it becomes moderate in February and March. It continues sometimes for six or nine successive days, and at other times blows only in the morning.

In the winter season violent tornadoes occur in May and June.

The great rains commence in July and last during August; and at the end of this month there is sometimes a return of tornadoes. The prevailing winds during this season are from S.W., light, and interrupted by calms; they sometimes blow strong from West. On this coast, while the fine season lasts, land and sea breezes blow alternately; the solar breezes are more regular, varying from N.N.E. to North in the morning, and from North to N.N.W. and N.W. in the evening. During the night the wind is light from East to E.N.E.

Cape Verd Islands.—Among the Cape Verd Islands from November to May, the Trade wind blows from N.E. to North or N.N.W. In the three first months of the year it is generally more from the North than on the coast of Senegal. In June it is from East and weaker. The rains begin about the end of this month. From July to October there are tornadoes, calms, and rain; at this period rollers are of frequent occurrence, especially at full and change. During the rainy season, from June to October, South winds are found, changing to S.E. and S.W., stormy, sometimes, with fog as well as calms and light baffling winds. The calms will depend much on the height of the land intercepting the Trade wind. After the 15th of August it is not prudent to remain in the bays of these islands, which are exposed to S.W. and S.E. winds.

Coast of Senegal.—On the coast of Senegal and between Cape Blanco and Cape Verd, winds from East to N.E. prevail from October to May, including eight months of the year. The winter season lasts from June till October, when tornadoes and light winds from S.W. to W.S.W. occur.

At a moderate distance from the coast, in the fine season, North winds are often found blowing on shore, while at the same time, further out at sea, the wind is from N.E. This coast is equally subject to the solar breezes, varying from N.E. to N.N.W. The breezes from N.N.W. prevail in the afternoon, hauling easterly in the night and towards morning.

Canary Isles.—In the archipelago of the Canaries

situated near the limit of the N.E. Trade winds, the winds blow from N.N.W. to N.N.E. by the North, during nearly the whole year, and particularly from April to October. From this last month also till February their direction is nearly the same. These winds are however interrupted by violent S.E. and S.W. winds, which last sometimes seven or eight following days in December to January, accompanied by much rain.

The roadsteads of the Canaries are dangerous during these winds, and they ought not to be visited at such periods. In the Grand Canary, the bay of Palmas is the only one which may be frequented without danger in December and January, because a ship can get under sail there with any wind.

These islands, like others of the Atlantic, are subject to variable winds. They have the alternate land and sea breeze, but from different directions according to local conditions. The calms occurring under these islands extend sometimes to forty leagues from them.

Madeira.—At Madeira the N.E. Trade wind becomes settled about the middle of April, and continues so till the end of September. In October the periodical rains may be expected, which commonly last for fifteen days. They frequently begin with a strong S.E. wind which changes to S.W., and continues to veer round to N.W., when the weather clears up. The roadstead of Funchal is very dangerous with these winds.

In November and December fine weather is found there, with the N.E. wind, which is yet irregular. January and February are the two months in which strong S.W. and South winds occur; but N.E. winds often blow during these months. In February sudden shifts of wind from E. to E.S.E. occur, followed by gales and rain. In March the prevalent winds are generally from N.W., and sometimes very strong, causing a heavy surf at Funchal. During this month a great deal of snow falls on the mountains of Madeira.

In April the weather is often bad until the middle of the month, and it sometimes blows very hard; but it is mostly fine in the beginning of this month. In May, June, and July, the nights are clear and the days cloudy. Regular land and sea breezes then prevail.

During August and part of September the harmattan, called by the inhabitants the East wind, sets in; it blows sometimes from the East, during six or nine days following, as it does on the coast of Morocco opposite Madeira.

CHAPTER IV.

Winds and Weather in the Strait of Gibraltar—Coast of Portugal—Bay of Biscay—Entrance of the Channel —British Isles—Holland—Norway.

The following remarks are worth preserving concerning the East wind at Gibraltar. They are from the Abstracts of Meteorological Observations taken at the stations of the Royal Engineers in 1852 and 1854.

If oil paint be laid on during a continuance of this wind it will not harden, but remain soft and sticky, or adhesive to everything laid upon it, and retains this quality for one or two years on a recurrence of easterly wind, even though apparently dry when the wind is West. It is commonly observed that meat will not keep during an East wind, * * * and has a great many other faults laid to its charge.

Winds and Weather in the Strait of Gibraltar.—From a series of observations made at Gibraltar and Cadiz during the six years from 1850 to 1855 it appears that easterly winds prevailed at Gibraltar during the months of July, August, September, December, and March; while at Cadiz easterly winds prevailed only in December. It also appears that at

Gibraltar and Cadiz, only a short distance apart, very different winds were blowing at the same time. Vessels are wrong, therefore, when bound to the West coast of Africa with westerly winds, to come to Gibraltar for an easterly wind to enable them to communicate with places on that coast. It would seem also that Cadiz, or even Tangier, would be better places for judging the weather of these parts than Gibraltar.

From these it appears that the proportion of westerly winds increases at Tangier, while that of easterly winds decreases. But easterly winds at Tangier are always prevalent in July, August, September, January, and March. Calms in the strait are very rare, and the wind is often strong.

The months of January, February, and March are generally bad for the navigation of the strait. About the end of October and November sometimes bad weather prevails in the strait, for it is the time of the short rainy season, which lasts from fifteen to twenty days.

In the winter months of January, February, and March, S.W. and S.E. gales are frequent, shifting to West and N.W. These gales, however, sometimes very heavy, do not last; but in February and March they follow each other at very short intervals. In the fine season from April to December inclusive, and even January, easterly and westerly winds prevail according to localities, under peculiar circumstances.

Peculiarities of the Wind in the Strait of Gibraltar.—In the Strait of Gibraltar the easterly winds have peculiarities very different from what is found with the same winds on the coast between Cape Trafalgar and Cadiz to the northward. There they come in squalls near the land, but in the strait are uniformly strong. In shore, and principally in the bays, a dead calm prevails both morning and evening; or the wind is light near the land, while outside it is blowing hard, especially in the middle of the strait, and one cannot tell from the anchorage the weather which prevails in the strait.

Easterly winds, instead of being dry, as they are on the coast between Cadiz and Trafalgar, are often very moist. They are attended with the mists of the shore, and the thicker the mist the harder is the wind. An abundance of dew, a mist over the land, and particularly spreading over the heights of Gibraltar —and especially over Apes Hill,—are all indications (and almost certain ones) of an approaching easterly wind; and they continue while it lasts.

During the fine season easterly winds are seldom attended with rain in the strait; but as they always bring more moisture to the eastern entrance of the strait than the western, it often happens that the collection of vapour which they form on the heights of Gibraltar and Apes Hill occasions rain at the foot of these mountains while there is fine weather in the strait. Again, in the fine season, and particularly in June, if, after a strong easterly wind, large white clouds are seen collected about the land in large masses, and if the S.W. or westerly wind comes in light airs, and a thick fog bank is formed in the western part of the strait, it gradually gains on the land and soon envelops the whole strait. These fogs are sometimes as thick and wet as those which are met with on the coast of Newfoundland in the month of August; but they are only of a few hours duration in the strait, and disappear as rapidly as they form.

Westerly Winds.—Still on this coast S.W. winds are the most dangerous. They are generally announced by a fall in the barometer, and commence from the southward. Very different from easterly winds, they take a certain time to become S.W., from whence they blow hardest. Like the S.W. winds of the Bay of Biscay, they shift suddenly to West, and even to N.W.; and if they continue at N.W. the weather becomes fine, but the squalls are heavy and sometimes stormy. These winds continue strong and generally go down at North. This character of the westerly wind specially applies to the winter. In the fine season of April and May these winds are generally moderate, bringing fine weather, although the sky may be overcast.

Westerly winds in the strait are generally moderate; in which case the sky is clear, and the land clear and remarkably distinct. If they freshen, the sky soon becomes overcast and squally with rain, attended by a considerable sea in the strait. Nevertheless, it may be said in general that westerly winds in the fine season (excepting a breeze now and then from the S.W., which will haul to West and N.W., and of very short duration) bring fine weather for navigation, and it is principally in October, November, and December that a gale occasionally comes from the westward.

Westerly winds which are attended with much moisture at the western entrance of the strait, are mostly dry at Gibraltar. And when the heights of Gibraltar and Apes Hill, after being covered with mist by a continuance of the easterly wind, become clear and conspicuous, it is a tolerably certain sign of a westerly wind being near.

Changes in the Strength and Direction of the Wind in the Strait.—In the fine season easterly winds in the strait are always fresh, while westerly winds there are mostly moderate. But easterly or westerly winds in the strait have this peculiarity, that in the vicinity of the coast they follow its direction. Thus, when the wind is due West in the strait, near the coast of Spain it becomes N.W., while near the African coast it is S.W. In like manner, easterly winds in the strait draw to the N.E. near the coast of Spain, and to S.E. near the coast of Africa.

But a remarkable fact which has been observed, and which is perhaps general in the strait, is that as the wind penetrates into the strait, it becomes stronger as it reaches its narrowest part. Thus, although the easterly wind may be light between Gibraltar and Ceuta, it blows hard between Tarifa and Point Ciris opposite, as well as in all the western part of the strait. And in the same manner westerly winds which are moderate between Trafalgar and Cape Spartel attain their greatest strength South of Tarifa, and preserve it in all the eastern part of the strait,—a peculiarity of which it is important the navigator should be informed.

S.W. Winds.—In the bad season, that is in February, March, and April, westerly winds come in squalls and are attended with heavy rain. In this season, also, easterly winds set in and veer S.E., accompanied by torrents of rain. The weather with them is nearly always murky and the sky overcast.

The worst winds of the strait are the S.W., and in the squalls by which they are attended they change suddenly to West, to N.W., and even to North, and sometimes N.N.E. When they remain between North and West, they generally lose their strength. The squalls which they bring generally are attended by rain and sometimes by hail. Between them there are intervals of fine weather, with moderate wind, and if this settles between N.W. and N.E., it goes down, and it clears up entirely. But if, on the contrary, after suddenly changing to N.W., the wind backs round again to S.W., it mostly redoubles its strength and brings rain in abundance.

N.W. and N.E. Winds.—N.W. and N.E. winds changing by the North are very rare in the strait; but when they come and are moderate they are attended with fine weather. In the bad season they blow with considerable force, but the pilots say that although N.W. winds may blow hard outside they are not much felt in Tangier Bay. In the bad season N.E. winds frequently bring rain, and when they veer to East or S.E. they generally freshen to a gale.

S.E. Winds.—The S.E. is the rainy wind of the strait, and is called the Levanter. These winds come with squalls, shifting suddenly to N.E. and even to

North. In these changes they blow hard all the time; but sometimes in changing to N.E. they moderate; but if they return again quickly to East or S.E., the bad weather will continue.

Peculiarities of the Wind on the Coast from Cadiz to Trafalgar.—On the coast between Cadiz and Cape Trafalgar easterly winds come in squalls, with a clear sky overhead. These are dry winds. Some small scanty white clouds (*cirrus*) are seen occasionally very high, but are soon dissipated; a white mist hangs over the land, thickening as it nears the horizon, and this state of things continues while the easterly wind lasts, and even indicates its approach.

The absence of dew and a bank of mist at sunrise and sunset are certain indications of an easterly wind.

In the fine weather season, while the easterly wind prevails, it is generally stronger and more persevering than the westerly wind. It will last for over a fortnight, blowing hard all the time. The native seamen say that it always blows for periods of three, six, or nine days. But, generally speaking, easterly winds will get up with considerable strength in a very short time; sometimes they freshen up to a gale in a very few hours.

In shore these winds often come in violent squalls, scarcely felt on deck, but severely so overhead and about the masts and rigging. They are very sudden in their visitations, without any warning, are hot, and leave off abruptly. But off shore these peculiarities are lost, and the breeze is steady and gradually goes down.

At Cadiz, easterly winds (called the Medina) often

blow strong; but in April, instead of being hot and dry, they are accompanied by heavy black clouds which often give rain and hail. They come in squalls, and often increase to gales. They will slacken in the evening to freshen in the morning; in the course of the day they are strong, and at night will come occasionally in sudden gusts.

Barometer.—In the course of the summer the changes of the barometer are almost nothing in the strait, but in winter time they seldom deceive. When it falls wind or rain may be expected. With northerly winds from N.N.W. to N.N.E. it is generally high, and keeps so with fresh N.E. winds, even when they bring rain. But as soon as the wind has any tendency to the southward it falls. S.W. and S.E. winds, being those which generally bring bad weather in the strait, are announced by a considerable fall in the barometer. But frequently this fall is only on account of rain, for, generally speaking, these changes of the barometer are more frequently followed by rain than by wind.

Seasons.—By observations made at Gibraltar and Cadiz, there appears to be considerable difference between the two places, as much in respect of rain as wind. For while at Gibraltar an average of sixty-eight days' rain are looked for every year, at Cadiz they have only eighteen. It is certain that often with S.W. winds rain falls at Tangier while it is dry at Gibraltar; and often while easterly winds bring rain in the eastern part of the strait it does not reach the western part.

It is generally considered that there are two rainy seasons in the strait. One of these, which commences sometimes in November and sometimes in December, or even in January, seldom lasts more than fifteen days. The weather afterwards becomes fine before the heavy winter rains, which sometimes last into May. In the years 1854 and 1855 the little rainy season occurred in November; December was dry: the rains recommenced in January and lasted through the first fortnight of April.

The months in which stormy weather is most common in the strait are those of September and October. Storms are not so common in April, May, and November, and rarely happen in the other months. They most frequently occur in the afternoon or again perhaps at night, when the weather is very uncertain and the wind very variable. Heavy gusts of wind, but of short duration, are experienced from opposite points, as from East and West, and clouds are seen, of different elevations, pursuing opposite directions, and this is a tolerably certain sign that the evening will not pass over without a storm.

In the months of September and October the pilots affirm that about fifteen or twenty miles outside the strait squally weather is met, with rain and most frequently attended with gales. The squalls, they say, are attended with a considerable quantity of rain and intervals of fine weather with calms or light winds. But it is prudent for ships under sail to be prepared for this weather, for when the wind of these squalls is strong, they assume something of the character of whirlwinds, and shift rapidly through four, six, or even eight points, blowing all the time the harder as the changes are more rapid and considerable.

In the Strait of Gibraltar, besides the sea produced by the wind then blowing, the ocean swell is also felt from beyond the strait, resulting from the wind prevailing there. But in proportion as these long seas penetrate into the strait, and especially if from the westward, they assume the direction of the coast, and run very differently from the direction they take from the wind outside. Thus with westerly winds varying from S.W. to N.W., in the bays on the African coast the sea appears to come from N.W., although the wind outside is S.W. The same with easterly winds varying to N.E. and S.E.; on the coast of Spain the sea comes from S.E., although often outside the wind producing it is N.E. The consequence is that neither on the African coast nor on the Spanish coast is there any really quiet anchorage where shelter is to be had. Another consequence is that if one attempts to judge the direction of the wind outside from the direction of the sea, one is led into all kinds of mistakes.

Whenever the ocean swell is observed in the strait as in the bays, whether from the N.E. or S.E., it is a sure indication of an approaching easterly wind; and the same may be said when it comes from N.W. or S.W. of a wind approaching from the westward.

While under sail in the strait with an easterly wind, it is necessary to be prepared for squalls, which are sometimes very heavy to the westward of the Rock of Gibraltar, in the vicinity of Apes Hill, as far as Point

Ciris, off Malabata, and in Tangier Bay, as well as to the West of Tarifa and anywhere near the coast of Spain between Cape Trafalgar and Cadiz.

In like manner, with westerly winds, squalls must be expected to the eastward of the Rock, also especially near the West shore of Algeciras Bay, crossing from the bay of Getares, and approaching Apes Hill, also in the bay of Benzus and Ceuta, as well as on the whole coast between Ceuta and Tetuan.

The easterly winds have been the subject of the following lines, attributed to the Hon. Mrs. George Wrottesley:—

You have heard of far-famed Gibraltar,
'Tis a wonderful place each one says;
I like it myself and don't falter
In adding my tribute of praise:
But take this advice, and don't quiz it,
If you value your comfort the least,
Do not fix on the time for your visit
When the wind is decidedly East.

Why do things turn all sour and musty?
And why has the mail not come in?
Why is everthing out of doors dusty?
And everything dripping within?
Why has such a one murdered his brother?
For these facts if a reason you'd find,
The same cause does for one as the other,
'Tis that horrible easterly wind!

Coast of Portugal.—On the coast of Portugal, and in general from Cape Finisterre to Cape St. Vincent during ten months of the year northerly winds prevail, varying from N.E. to N.N.W. They blow fresh with fine weather, especially during summer, at which season there is generally a haze over the land with a N.E. wind. Winter gales come most frequently from South or S.W., sometimes from W.S.W., and blow very hard. If calms occur in winter after S.W. winds, bad weather will probably follow, and gales are generally preceded by a swell.

From Cape St. Vincent to the Canary Isles, the prevailing winds are from N.E. to N.W.

Bay of Biscay.—In the Bay of Biscay the wind is most variable; but it has been observed that in the winter months it varies from S.W. to N.W. by the West, the last being the most frequent. From May to September, sometimes also in December and January, winds from E.N.E., East, and E.S.E. are found. During the two last-mentioned months, these winds are fresh and lasting; those from N.E. freshening up with rain, and if there is a gale of wind it will come from East or S.E. and may be expected to be severe.

On the coast of Brittany S.W. winds prevail; weak in summer, but violent in winter, and changing from West to N.W., from whence heavy storms and gales of wind may be expected.

At the entrance of the Channel and on the West coast of France, the prevailing winds are generally from S.W. varying to West, W.N.W., and N.W. They last very long, blowing for seven or eight months, and freshen into violent gales, especially in winter. The wind from W.S.W. and S.W. is generally accompanied by rain or fog, while from N.W. it is stormy, but attended frequently with a clear sky.

Should the N.W. wind be moderate it is generally attended with fine weather interrupted however in winter by storms of considerable violence attended with hail and thunder. On the West coast of France these are commonly called "sea storms." These winds may be relied on more than any others. They sometimes originate in northern America, and traverse the whole Atlantic Ocean.

In summer S.W. winds prevail, alternately moderate and fresh with foul weather. However, in this season the sky is generally clear with a S.W. wind.

In this season, if the wind is S.W. and the weather fine, if it veers to N.W. it generally strengthens, but the weather will still continue fine.

Strong S.W. and N.W. Winds in the Bay of Biscay.—In the English Channel or Bay of Biscay, when the wind comes in squalls from the S.W., whether in summer or winter, if it be attended by rain, increasing in quantity, and the squalls become heavier and more frequent, with a slight tendency to vary, a change of wind may be expected. Generally the change is from S.W. to West rapidly, and sometimes to N.W. in a squall, and blowing harder than before. This state of weather may become of serious consequence to ships working to windward and on the port tack, and even to those running free or with the wind abaft, if unprepared and sail be not reduced in time.

Sometimes the change from S.W. to N.W. is preceded by a short calm, which must never be trusted. It has also been observed in the Bay of Biscay that when a breeze springs up from a point opposite to the sun, it does not last, and indicates merely a slight derangement of the atmosphere.

Winds fròm North and South.—Winds from North and South are not very frequent; they prevail now and then, but not to a great extent nor for a long interval, although they sometimes freshen up into strong breezes and even gales. Those from South will draw to S.E. or S.W.; and those from North will become N.E. or N.W.

Entrance of the Channel.—At the entrance of the Channel, although the wind is very changeable, it is found that westerly winds are most prevalent in September, October, and November; and easterly winds in December, January, and February.

Of the winds of the English Channel little need be said, for in any season of the year their direction and force is most uncertain. It has been determined, however, that the westerly winds (and those southward of West) predominate so much as to nearly double those from the eastward in the course of the year. And it is also commonly observed that the South is the rainy quarter, the North mostly dry. If it blow fresh from S.E. or S.W. or any point between, it is either sure to be accompanied by moisture, either in haze, a drizzling rain, or if not constant wet,—the whole atmosphere being loaded with vapour, and the barometer generally low. But with the wind from N.W. to N.E. or any intermediate point, even if fresh there is much more chance of the weather being fine and dry. If from the N.W., the clouds that may be about will assume compact well-defined forms, generally well rounded and packed close together, leaving abundant intervals between of blue sky, the atmosphere at the same time being clear, with a healthy, exhilarating air: barometer high. The same from the North may be looked for, but if the wind freshens and becomes squally, rain (or snow in winter) follows, and from the N.E. it will be cloudy, the entire atmosphere being overcast, as well as from the S.E.

Calms in the Channel occur at all times of the year, and generally precede a change of wind, especially if it has been long from any one quarter.

Easterly winds do not commence suddenly. When likely to last they begin with light airs from a calm; perhaps the last of a westerly wind may be blowing light overhead, while below it a light air, at first scarcely perceptible, will gradually be coming on from the East. The easterly wind will be accompanied for some days with an overcast sky, which will gradually clear away, and it will freshen considerably, still remaining easterly, without rain, all the time with a high barometer.

It has also been observed that spring tides bring a westerly wind with them on the flood coming up Channel, and if blowing fresh mostly are attended with rain. Those gales of autumn or winter which come on from the S.W., frequently in the course of a few hours haul round by the North to N.E., gradually subsiding while they are drawing round.

British Isles.—On the shores of the British Isles, the prevailing winds are nearly the same as those in the Bay of Biscay. It is, however, observed that in Scotland, North winds are very frequent, and that East winds blow principally from March to June. In England and Ireland South and S.W. winds prevail; and it is observed that on the coast of Cornwall westerly winds blow during nearly nine months of the year.

Coast of Holland.—On the coast of Holland westerly winds prevail, attended by rain and fog. Winds from S.E., South, and N.W. seldom blow, but from S.W. they do frequently; easterly winds, which occur in every month of the year, prevail in the four winter months, producing dry cold weather.

Coast of Norway.—On the western coast of Norway the prevailing winds are from S.W. to South, frequently attended by rain.

CHAPTER V.

American Coast—Arctic—Newfoundland—Gulf and River St. Lawrence—Sable Island—Nova Scotia—Bay of Fundy—United States.

Greenland.—Greenland cannot boast a periodic wind. From May to July the weather is fine, the wind changeable, but most frequently very strong from S.S.W. Even until September the winds are variable, but rain is by no means frequent. Storms seldom occur, and when they do are of short duration. The most violent squalls come from South. The coldest winds are from N.E., and this may form the sum total of our remarks on Greenland.

Arctic Region in North America.—In the following table we have resumed the observations on winds collected by Captain Parry in his voyage to the Arctic regions to discover a passage from the Atlantic to the Pacific Ocean. These observations are doubly interesting since they are continued without interruption from July, 1819, to September, 1820; consequently showing the prevailing winds of these frozen regions during more than a year. This table is only a summary of those published in Captain Parry's voyage,

Month.	North.	N.N.W.	N.W.	W.N.W.	West.	W.S.W.	S.W.	S.S.W.	South.	S.S.E.	S.E.	E.S.E.	East.	E.N.E.	N.E.	N.N.E.	Calm.	Variable.	General Remarks.
1819. July ..	3	5½	3	..	4½	..	2½	..	1	2½	3	..	2	..	..	1½	2½	..	E. and S., fresh, with rain; the other breezes light; much mist and fog; snow with N. wind.
Aug. ..	4	..	5	..	1½	..	6	..	2	½	1½	..	4	..	2½	1½	1	1½	Strong E. winds and fog; N., moderate, cloudy; S.W., rain; N.N.W., fresh, cloudy, misty.
Sept. ..	7	4	4	..	3½	..	5½	..	..	..	..	..	..	..	1½	4½	..	..	Strong W. in gusts; N.N.E., fresh, misty; snow with strong N. wind; other breezes moderate.
Oct. ..	10½	7½	1	..	5½	..	3	..	..	1	..	..	1	..	1	..	..	½	Strong N., weather clear, fine; N.W., fresh, cloudy; W., fr., snow, fog; S.W., st., misty; E., st., snow.
Nov. ..	16	6	1	..	1½	..	1½	..	..	1	..	..	..	..	..	..	1	2	N., moderate, fine, snow, hurricanes; S.W., fine; other breezes light or moderate.
Dec. ..	5½	3	5	..	2	1	½	..	3½	..	1	3½	5	..	..	..	..	1	E., fresh, weather cloudy; mist and fog with S.
1820. Jan. ..	11½	7½	½	..	4½	..	..	..	..	1	1½	1	2½	..	..	1	½	..	S.S.E., st., fine weather; N. and N.N.W., st., or fr., fine; much fog during this month.
Feb. ..	9	9	..	..	3	..	..	..	1	..	1	..	1	..	..	..	2	3	N.N.W., strong; N., fresh, much fog.
March.	17½	4	2½	..	2	..	..	..	1	½	..	1	..	..	..	..	..	2	N., fr., weather clear, some snow; S., clear; W., fr.
April..	9½	4	3	..	..	..	..	..	..	½	1	2	2½	..	..	1½	1	5	N.N.W., fr.; N., light, snow, fine; E., fr., snow.
May ..	11	3	5	½	..	..	..	..	4	½	..	1	1	..	1	..	3	1	N. and N.N.W., strong, alternate clear and cloudy weather; squalls from N.W.
June ..	7	2½	2	..	4	..	..	2½	2	1	3½	..	1½	..	..	..	..	5	N., st., fine, cloudy, rain, fog, snow for two days.
Total..	111½	56	32	½	32	1	19	2½	14½	8½	12½	8½	19½	..	6	10	11	21	
July ..	9	1	1	3	1½	..	1½	1	4	2	1	..	..	..	..	3	..	3	N., fr., cloudy; S., fr., rain.; S.S.W., st., freq. fog.
Aug. ..	1½	1	3	8	8½	3	..	1	..	..	..	2	1½	1	..	..	1½	5	W.N.W., N.N.W., E.S.E., fr., snow, fog, often cloudy.
Sept. ..	1	2½	4½	1	1½	2	1	..	4	1	5	..	1	..	2½	1½	..	..	S.W., strong, seven days snow, mist, fog; varying breezes, fresh, and often in gusts.
Total..	11½	4½	8½	7	11½	5	2½	2	8	3	6	2	2½	1	2½	4½	1½	8	

The figures indicate the number of days during which the wind has blown from the quarter stated in the first horizontal column.

who from September, 1819, till August, 1820, remained between the parallels of 74° and 75° North latitude.

Summary of observations made on board the *Hecla* during an interval of twelve months, in which period the vessel was in the latitudes of 74° and 75° N.

Months.	Thermometer.			Barometer.		
	Max.	Min.	Mean.	Max.	Min.	Mean.
819.	°	°	°			
September....	+37	— 1	+22·54	30·42	29·63	29·90
October	+17·5	—28	— 8·46	30·32	29·36	29·81
November	+ 6	—47	—29·60	30·32	29·10	29·94
December	+ 6	—43	—21·79	30·75	29·10	29·86
1820.						
January	— 2	—47	—30·09	30·77	29·59	30·07
February	—17	—50	—32·19	30·15	29·32	29·76
March........	+ 6	—40	—18·10	30·26	29·00	29·80
April	+32	—32	— 8·37	30·86	29·40	29·97
May..........	+47	— 4	+16·60	30·48	29·25	30·10
June	+51	+28	+36·24	30·13	29·50	29·82
July..........	+60	+32	+42·41	31·01	29·13	29·66
August	+45	+22	+32·68	30·03	29·46	29·73

Remarks.—The thermometer when placed on shore or on the ice at a distance from the ship invariably stood from 3° to 4° or 5°, and even on some occasions 7° lower than on board. The mean temperature for the year may therefore be fairly considered as —2°. The lowest temperature registered on the ice was —55°; it did not rise above —54° for seventeen hours on the 14th and 15th of February, 1820.

The two preceding tables conclude the observations on the Arctic region of North America, and, in order to render them as complete as possible, we further give the table of observations also made by Captain Parry in his third voyage to discover the North West passage. These observations embrace a period of sixteen months—from June, 1824, to September, 1825.

Observations made at Port Bowen in lat. 73° 49′ N. and long. 87° 25′ W.

Month	North.	N.E.	East.	S.E.	South.	S.W.	West.	N.W.	Var.	Calms.	Remarks on the Weather.
1824-5											
June	½	2	11	1	8½	3	...	2	2	...	Much fog and rain; fine with E. wind.
July	9½	5	½	5	2½	1½	1½	5½	...	...	Wind variable and weak; foggy.
Aug.	3½	1½	3	7	3½	2½	1½	7	1½	...	Remarkable for rain and snow.
Sept.	1½	1½	4½	9	...	2	9	1½	...	1	Breezes fresh and gusty.
Oct.	4	2½	10½	6½	1	...	½	5	1	...	Fresh E. breezes; snow and fog.
Nov.	2	...	8½	8	...	2½	1½	5½	2	...	Wind by gusts; clear with N.W. wind.
Dec.	4	1	15	4½	...	1	1½	2	2	...	Fine with E. wind; clear, a little snow.
Jan.	8	2½	18	1½	...	...	...	8	3	...	Very fine month; few storms.
Feb.	3	2	18½	...	...	...	1	2½	...	1	Ditto.
Mar.	...	½	18	...	...	2	2	7½	1	...	Fine; some storms.
April	2½	...	18	2	...	...	4	2½	1	...	Fine; a few storms; a little snow during five days.
May	3	3	9½	1	3	1	2	7½	1	...	Strong breezes from S.E.; dull weather, squalls, snow.
June	1½	1	12½	2½	2	4½	2½	8½	...	...	Stormy; wind variable; misty.
July	4	1	...	5	2½	3	12	4	...	...	Weather generally cloudy.
Aug.	9	8½	1	...	1½	2½	1½	7	...	...	Cloudy, mist, rain, light breezes.
Sept.	1½	3	3½	1	5½	3	4½	8	...	...	Cloudy, rain, fog, light breezes.
Total	52½	35	158	54	30	28	45	74	14½	2	

This may conclude the Arctic observations with the remark that in the Arctic regions the winds are most variable and irregular; while they are generally moderate in all seasons of the year.

The subsequent Arctic voyages of the *Alert* and *Discovery*, the *Vega*, and other expeditions have been the means of obtaining much valuable information, but it is hardly within the scope of this work to enter into further details of these regions.

Hudson Bay.—In Hudson Bay it is observed that from October to May the prevailing winds are from North to N.W., and from June to October from S.E. to East. The northerly winds are very strong, and in spring and autumn squally, tempestuous weather is most common.

Canada.—According to some writers, we find in

Canada winds blowing regularly from North during five winter months. According to others, N.E. and S.W. winds prevail alternately; the former at the end of autumn and during winter. From December to April, the weather is generally serene. The occasional N.W. winds which blow at this period are colder than those from N.E., and are common while the ice lasts. They are only met at sea in these regions about the month of March. They increase in June, and afterwards gradually diminish. The following table contains a summary of the winds observed during the year 1834 in Lower Canada.

Months.	Winds.	Remarks on the Weather.
January ..	W.N.W.	Weather generally fine.
February..	W. and E.N.E.	Much snow.
March....	W. and E.	Snow and rain.
April	Variable.	Generally fine.
May	Ditto.	Ditto.
June	Ditto.	Ditto.
July	Ditto.	Ditto.
August ..	Ditto.	Ditto.
September	Ditto.	Rain and cloudy weather.
October ..	E.N.E.	Snow and rain.
November.	S.S.E.	Snow.
December.	W.N.W.	Variable.

Newfoundland.—On the East and South coast of the island of Newfoundland the winds most generally found are from South from May till October. They are, however, very changeable, and generally moderate during this period. Nevertheless, there are occasional squalls from S.E., with rain and fog: which latter is especially prevalent in July and August. The N.W. winds which occasionally blow are dry and cold, and generally attended with a clear sky. In October these winds become violent. S.W. winds are also found here, but very variable in strength, at all times of the year.

Gulf and River St. Lawrence.—Fogs.—Fogs may occur at any time during the open or navigable season, but are most frequent in the early part of summer; they are rare and never of long continuance during westerly winds, but seldom fail to accompany an easterly wind of any strength or duration. The above general observation is subject, however, to restriction, according to locality or season. Thus winds between the South and West, which are usually clear weather winds above Anticosti, are frequently accompanied with fog in the eastern parts of the gulf. Winds between the South and East are almost always accompanied with rain and fog in every part. E.N.E. winds above Point de Monts are often E.S.E. or S.E. winds in the gulf, changed in direction by the high lands of the South coast, and have therefore in general the same foggy character. Winds of considerable strength and duration are here meant, and which probably extend over great distances. Moderate and partial fine weather winds may occur without fog at any season and in any locality. In the early part of the navigable season, especially in the months of April and May, clear weather N.E. winds are of frequent occurrence, and they also sometimes occur at other seasons, in every part of the gulf and river.

The fogs sometimes last several days in succession, and to a vessel either running up or beating down, during their continuance, there is no safe guide but the constant use of the deep sea lead, with a chart containing correct soundings.

The fogs which accompany easterly gales extend high up into the atmosphere, and cannot be looked over from any part of the rigging of a ship. They, however, are not so thick as those which occur in calms after a strong wind, and which are frequently so dense as to conceal a vessel within hail; whilst the former often, but not always, admit the land, or other objects to be distinguished at the distance of half a mile or more in the daytime.

The dense fogs, which occur in calms, or even in very light winds, often extend only to small elevations above the sea; so that it sometimes happens that when objects are hidden at the distance of fifty yards from the deck, they can be plainly seen by a person fifty or sixty feet up the rigging. In the months of October and November the fogs and rain that accompany easterly gales, are replaced by thick snow, which causes equal embarrassment to the navigator.

Winds.—The prevailing winds during the navigable season are either directly up or directly down the estuary, following the course of the chains of high lands on either side of the great valley of the St. Lawrence. Thus a S.E. wind in the gulf becomes E.S.E. between Anticosti and the South coast, E.N.E. above Point de Monts, and N.E. above Green Island. The westerly winds do not appear to be so much guided in direction by the high lands, excepting along the South coast, where we have observed a W.S.W.

wind at the island of Bic become West, N.N.W., and N.W., as we ran down along the high and curved South coast, until it became a N.N.W. wind at Cape Gaspé. These winds frequently blow strong for three or four days in succession; the westerly winds being almost always accompanied with fine, dry, clear, and sunny weather; the easterly winds as frequently the contrary, cold, wet, and foggy.

In the spring, the easterly winds mostly prevail, frequently blowing for several weeks in succession. As the summer advances, the westerly winds become more frequent, and the S.W. winds take place occasionally; but North winds are not common in summer, although they sometimes occur. Steady N.W. winds do not blow frequently before September, excepting for a few hours at a time, when they generally succeed easterly winds which have died away to a calm, forming the commencement of strong winds, and usually veering to the S.W. The N.W. wind is dry, with bright clear sky, flying clouds, and showers. After the autumnal equinox, winds to the northward of West become more common, and are then often strong steady winds of considerable duration. In the months of October and November, the N.W. wind frequently blows with great violence in heavy squalls, with passing showers of hail and snow, and attended with sharp frost.

Thunderstorms are not uncommon in July and August; they seldom last above an hour or two; but the wind proceeding from them is in general violent and sudden, particularly when near the mountainous part of the coast; sail should, therefore, be fully and quickly reduced on their approach.

Strong winds seldom veer quickly from one quarter of the compass to another directly or nearly contrary; in general they die away by degrees to a calm, and are succeeded by a wind in the opposite direction. It is not meant, however, by this observation that they may not veer to the amount of several points. N.W. winds seldom or never veer round by North and N.E. to East and S.E.; but they do frequently, by degrees, to the S.W., after becoming moderate. S.W. winds seldom veer by the N.W. and North to the eastward, but sometimes by the South to S.E. and East. Easterly winds generally decrease to a calm, and are succeeded by a wind from the opposite direction.

In the fine weather westerly winds of summer, a fresh top-gallant breeze will often decrease to a light breeze or calm at night, and spring up again from the same quarter on the following morning; under these circumstances only may a land breeze off the North coast be looked for. The same has been observed off the South coast also, but not so decidedly or extending so far off shore. The North land wind may occasionally be carried nearly over to the South coast just before daylight, but the South land wind seldom extends more than five or six miles off, and that very rarely. Under the same circumstances, that is with a fine weather westerly wind going down with the sun, a S.W. land breeze will frequently be found blowing off the North coast of Anticosti at night and during the early part of the morning. If, however, the weather be not settled fair, and the wind does not fall with the sun, it will usually prove worse than useless to run a vessel close in shore at night in the hope of a breeze off the land.

Such is the usual course of the winds in common seasons, in which a very heavy gale of wind will probably not be experienced from May to October, although close-reefed topsail breezes are usually common enough. Occasionally, however, there are years the character of which is decidedly stormy. Gales of wind of considerable strength then follow each other in quick succession and from opposite quarters.

Barometer.—The marine barometer, which is at all times of great use to the navigator, becomes particularly so in such seasons; and the following remarks upon its general indications, when taken in connection with the usual course of the winds and weather of the St. Lawrence, may, therefore, be useful. The barometer has ordinarily a range from 29 to 30·5 inches in the gulf and river during the navigable season, and its changes accompany those of the winds and weather with a considerable degree of constancy. The fluctuations of the barometric column are much greater and more frequent there than in lower latitudes; and sudden alternations, which in other climates would be alarming, may occur there without being followed by any corresponding change either in the wind or weather. But the navigator should not be inattentive to those minor changes, as a constant attention to the instrument can alone enable him to appreciate those decisive indications of the mercury which seldom or never prove deceptive. The following remarks will apply to those well marked changes which usually indicate the approach of a gale of considerable strength, or of a shift of wind and weather; the correct anticipation of which is often of the utmost consequence to the safety of a vessel, as well as to the length of her voyage.

When, after a continuance of westerly winds and fine weather, the barometer has risen nearly to its greatest height, say some tenths above 30 inches, or begins to fall a little, an easterly wind may be soon expected. If to this notice given by the barometer be added a warm, hazy atmosphere during the day, and a heavy precipitation of dew at night, with very bright twinkling stars, or a coloured aurora borealis, the approach of a southerly or easterly wind is almost certain. If land be in sight at such a time, and appears much distorted by terrestrial refraction, or if vessels in sight have the relative proportions of their hull and sails changed by the *mirage*, or present double or treble images, such appearances will render the before probable indications of the barometer certain. At the commencement the southerly or easterly wind will probably be light with fine clear weather, but this will not last above a few hours if the barometer continues to fall; on the contrary the wind will gradually increase, and as it does so the sky will become overcast by degrees until it is completely clouded. Rain and fog will follow, and continue during the continuance of the southerly or easterly wind with little intermission, until they are dissipated by a fresh breeze from the contrary quarter.

If the fall of the barometer, during the continuance of the southerly or easterly wind, be very slow, the gale will probably continue, and not be violent: if rapid, it will probably be of short duration, and of greater strength: at any rate, when the mercury falls towards 29 inches a change is certainly at hand, and the gale will in general come from the N.W. The strength of this succeeding gale will be in proportion to the fall of the barometer, and to the strength of the southerly or easterly gale which preceded it. In such a case there is seldom many hours' interval between the one gale and the other. The southerly or easterly wind generally dies away to calm, and in a very few hours, or sometimes in much less time, the N.W. gale springs up. A heavy cross sea remains for some time from the previous gale.

The barometer sometimes begins to rise in the interval of the calm which precedes the N.W. gale, at others at its commencement: the fog and rain cease, and the weather becomes quite clear, generally in a few hours, and sometimes almost immediately. The strength of the westerly gale is usually greatest soon after its commencement, and diminishes as the barometer rises, veering gradually to the West and S.W. It is worthy of remark that the circumstances just mentioned are exactly the reverse of those attending the easterly gale. The latter usually commences with clear weather and a high barometer, light at first from the South or S.E., and gradually increasing as it veers to the eastward, with a falling barometer.

To return to the westerly gale. If, after it has veered to S.W. and become moderate, the barometer remains steady at a moderate height, fine weather may be expected. If it remains at a considerable height, but still fluctuating and unsteady, within certain limits, variable, but not heavy winds, and variable weather may be expected. If, on the contrary, it rises quickly to a great height a repetition of the southerly or easterly gale will not be improbable. Seasons have been experienced in which the barometer may be said to have been no sooner blown up by one wind, than it has been blown down by another, and this stormy alternation to have continued for several months; whilst in others there has been scarcely a double-reefed topsail breeze during the whole summer.

There is in fact so great a difference in the phenomena of the weather in different seasons, that it becomes difficult to write anything respecting it that shall not be liable to many exceptions. There are, however, some strongly marked cases of connection between the indications of the barometer and changes of the winds and weather which have been subject to few, or almost no exceptions. The first of these cases is that most common one, of a southerly or an easterly gale, with a falling barometer, being always wet and foggy, and succeeded by a strong wind from the opposite quarter, with a rising barometer, and fine weather. A second case, not of so frequent occurrence in common seasons, excepting in spring or early in summer, is the N.E. wind with a rising barometer, which, although it may not be at first for a few hours, will almost always become fine and clear, and end in fine weather. A third case may be considered certain: if the barometer fall suddenly and greatly at any time, a northerly and most probably a N.W. gale of great strength may be confidently expected. It does not follow that it will be immediate, for it may be preceded by a strong gale from S.W. for a few hours, during which the barometer will seldom rise, and even, probably, continue to fall; but when the South-west gale dies away the northerly or North-west winds will soon succeed, with a rising barometer.

In conclusion, it may be remarked that as, on the one hand, a considerable fall of the barometer may occur without being followed by a strong wind, so, on the other, a breeze of considerable strength may come on without any indication from the barometer; but not anything that deserves the name of a gale. There has never, within our experience, occurred a gale so heavy as to be of serious consequence to a good vessel, the approach of which has not been indicated by the barometer. But it must be remembered that a high barometer in this climate, and under the circumstances which have been mentioned, is often indicative of a southerly or an easterly gale. It is remarkable that in the gulf and estuary of the St. Lawrence a high barometer may be considered as the forerunner of wet and foggy weather, which usually accompanies its fall; whilst a low barometer renders it equally probable that dry weather will ensue, since it as often accompanies its rise. The marine barometer, therefore, is of the greatest assistance in the navigation of the gulf and river; and by attending constantly to its state and changes, with reference to the winds and weather which preceded them, combined with the indications afforded by the appearance of the sky, &c., those changes of the wind and weather which are about to take place may be anticipated with a degree of certainty, sufficient, in most cases, to enable a vessel to avoid being caught on a lee shore or in an unsafe anchorage, as well as to regulate her course in anticipation of the coming change.

Sable Island.—The climate of Sable Island appears to be greatly influenced by its proximity to the Gulf Stream, which is distant from it only about seventy miles to the southward. Winds from that direction almost immediately dissolve the snow which had previously fallen; causing, with the alternating northerly winds, a wider range and yet a higher mean temperature than occurs on the neighbouring continent during the winter months. The southerly winds coming thus from a warm to a comparatively cold sea, are compelled to part with a portion of their moisture, and hence are almost always accompanied with a dense fog.

These winds greatly prevail during the summer months, the S.W. especially, and the sand of the island thus copiously supplied with moisture, and heated at the same time by a powerful sun, is enabled to support an amount and variety of vegetation not usually found in such situations.

The barometer seldom or never rises with these winds, and when it falls with them rapidly and extensively, rain and wind, and if it be after the middle of August, a heavy gale may be expected.

Winds from between the North and East prevail most during spring and early summer. They are sometimes, and especially when from near the North, accompanied by the fine weather that usually attends the rising barometer ; but at other times, and almost always in autumn and winter, the easterly winds bring bad weather and are accompanied by a falling barometer.

Some of the heaviest gales in these seas have been from this quarter, and they are usually followed, almost immediately after the barometer has reached its lowest point of depression, by an equally strong gale from between the North and West, and which is always accompanied by clear weather and a rising barometer.

Easterly as well as southerly winds are foggy. The latter became less predominant as the summer advances, when westerly winds and clear weather become proportionately of less rare occurrence.

It is the fogs, even more than the irregular tides and currents, that render this island so dangerous : they frequently last many days and nights in succession with the prevalent easterly and southerly winds of early summer ; and even as late as the beginning of August, when we were about the island, only six days out of nineteen were entirely free from fogs. Winds between the North and West are, in general frequent in autumn and winter. They almost always bring fine clear weather, with a rising barometer; but they are often of great strength and in winter accompanied with intense frost.

Nova Scotia.—On the coast of Nova Scotia S.W. winds are nearly constant, and when blowing fresh frequently are accompanied by fog. In summer they become more southerly, but still fog prevails and is only cleared away with the wind from the West or northward of West. In winter time the northerly and N.W. winds are attended with sharp, clear, cold weather. When the wind is light, the weather is usually fine, although cold; but when blowing fresh and stormy, with snow, is very trying to navigators.

The following is a summary of observations of the winds at Halifax on the East coast of Nova Scotia.

Months.	Winds.	Remarks on the Weather.
January ..	N., S., and W.	Clear, rain, snow.
February ..	N.W. and var.	Clear, rain, cloudy.
March	N.W. and S.W.	Ditto.
April......	West.	Ditto.
May	North and West.	Clear and rain at intervals.
June	W., N., and N.W.	Ditto.
July	W., N., and S., var.	Clear and misty.
August....	W. and S., var.	Clear, cloudy, rain, mist.
September..	N.W. and S., var.	Ditto.
October....	S.W., N., and N.W.	Clear.
November..	West and S.W.	Clear, rain, mist.
December..	N.W. and N.E.	Clear and rain.

New Brunswick.—In New Brunswick the following observations have been made at Fredericton, the capital of this colony, by Sir James MacGregor.

Months.	East.	South	West.	North	Var.	Fine.	Rain.	Mist.	Snow.
January ...	4	...	7	6	14	24	2	1	4
February ...	2	4	4	2	16	23	1	...	4
March	23	2	5	...	1	22	2	2	5
April.........	12	4	11	...	3	22	7	...	1
May	20	1	7	...	3	18	8	5	...
June.........	19	1	10	...	...	15	6	9	...
July	20	...	7	2	2	18	3	10	...
August	17	...	9	4	1	23	3	5	...
September..	17	...	10	2	1	17	5	8	...
October......	14	...	8	...	9	22	7	2	...
November..	11	5	...	14	...	15	8	3	4
December...	...	...	9	14	8	26	...	2	3
Total...	159	17	87	44	58	245	52	47	21

East Coast of North America.—On the East coast of North America the winds are neither constant nor uniform. In winter they are generally from N.W., and are most frequently dry. Winds from East, E.S.E., and S.E., produce rain, and the latter often very heavy.

Cape Hatteras is celebrated for the constant bad weather prevalent during the greater part of the year. On this coast, says Franklin, hurricanes from N.E. are found; they first visit the S.W. part of the United States, in Georgia, and from thence pass successively over the country in their progress to the North, sometimes reaching Newfoundland. These violent winds last sometimes for two or three days, accompanied by rain and dense clouds.

CHAPTER VI.

West Indies—Bahamas—Florida—Gulf of Mexico—Northers, Vera Cruz—Yucatan—Antilles—Porto Bello—Cartagena.

Bahamas.—In the Bahama Channel the Trade wind from N.E. in winter is interrupted by North winds and in summer by calms. In winter, that is to say, from November to April, we find winds changing from East to South, and from South to West. In December and January there are frequently North winds, changing to N.W., blowing violently for seven or eight consecutive days.

In summer, from May to September, the prevailing winds of the Bahama Channel are from S.E. to S.W. by the South. During March and April southerly winds are frequent.

East Coast of Florida.—From the parallel of 28° North latitude to the Florida Cays, the Trade wind blows till noon, and shortly after is followed by the sea breeze. This takes place regularly during summer; in winter, principally from November to March, the winds blow from South to West, and bring a heavy sea.

West Coast of Florida.—On the West coast of Florida, even as far as 28° North latitude, alternate land and sea breezes prevail.

Gulf of Mexico.—In the interior of the Gulf of Mexico the Trade winds are generally found, but near the coast only in proportion as the local winds there diminish their force.

The most violent of these are called *Huesos Colorados;* the more moderate *Chocolateros;* and they are found as far as the Bahama Channel. The Northers of the Gulf of Mexico are announced by a heavy swell getting up in the Bay of Campeche, by considerable humidity in the atmosphere, and by a dark cloud appearing in the N.W. in the morning and evening, keeping 9° or 10° above the horizon, for two or three days sometimes, before the Norther arrives. Lightning North-west and North-east, and gossamer floating in the air and hanging in the rigging, called *hilos de la vierga;* all these, as well as the phosphorescence of the sea, are indications of the approaching Norther. The wind commences first with a light air from South,—and then passes the round of the compass by West, and when it arrives at N.N.W., blows with all its violence. These gales, which are very dangerous in the Gulf of Mexico, generally last two or three days. When the wind is N.W., if the black cloud above mentioned begins to disappear, the gale will last but a short time, and the wind, which is then much less, hauls to the East, and if it becomes N.E., the weather moderates. They are often attended with much rain, and heavy cloudy weather, and cause a very heavy sea.

Dry Season.—The Northers of the Gulf of Mexico prevail from the middle of September to March, which is the dry season. In October they are stronger than at other times, and if they are not found at this period, the Trade winds are interrupted by storms and rain. In November the Northers are quite settled, with considerable strength, and continue during December, January, and February. In March and even April, when they become light, they are then stronger at daybreak than in the preceding months; they also *veer to the N.W.* Maury gives the following account of these winds. He says:

"They prevail from November to March, and commence with the thermometer about 80° or 85°. A calm ensues on the coast; black clouds roll up from the North; the wind is heard several minutes before it is felt; the thermometer begins to fall; the cold Norther bursts upon the people, bringing the temperature down to 28° and sometimes to 25°, before the inhabitants have time to change clothing and make fires. So severe is the cold, so dry the air, that men and cattle have been known to perish in them. These are the winds which, entering the gulf and sucking up heat and moisture therefrom, still retain enough of strength to make themselves terrible to mariners,—they are the far famed Northers of Vera Cruz."

Damp Season, or Season of the Trade Winds.—The damp season on the coast of the Gulf of Mexico, prevails from March to September. From the end of March and during April the Trade winds from E.S.E., interrupted occasionally by North winds, are sometimes attended with a clear sky, at other times with a sky overcast; they veer to S.E. and last all night. From

July to October violent storms, accompanied by thunder, lightning, and heavy rains, are frequently experienced. Those from East are the most severe, but of the least duration.*

Hurricane Season.—The period of hurricanes in the Gulf of Mexico, like the Antilles, is principally from August to October; † and the rainy season, called the winter in these regions, like the opposite on the coast of Africa, commences when the sun reaches the zenith of the place, passing to the North; and terminates when it again reaches the zenith of the same place, passing to the South.

Pensacola.—At Pensacola, chiefly from April to July, in the morning the wind is from North to East, or from East to South, followed in the afternoon by the wind from S.W. These S.W. winds (from sea) are termed *Virazones;* they blow in squalls in August, September, and October, a period when hurricanes are also experienced. From November to March northerly winds prevail; they begin at S.E. and South, with much rain; then veer to S.W. and West, at which point they remain some time, blowing very strong till they shift to N.W. and North; the weather then becomes fine.

Coasts from the Mississippi to the Bay of San Bernardo.—From the mouth of the Mississippi to the Bay of San Bernardo, land breezes prevail about daybreak

* Bernardo de Orta: *Derrotero de las Antillas.*

† We do not allude now to the hurricanes of the Atlantic Ocean. In the Indian Ocean we have collected all the facts relative to these terrible phenomena, and pointed out the laws of their progress. See *Storm Compass: by A. B. Becher, Captain, R.N.*, published by Potter, 31, Poultry.

from April to August. A short time after daybreak the wind veers to East and S.E., and blows from S.W. in the afternoon. In July, August, and September, squalls are frequent, with rain; there are, besides, southerly winds, changing from South to S.W. in squalls, which last several successive days. The worst months for navigating this coast, are those of August, September, October, and November, because then the winds are severe, and blow dead on shore, without permitting a vessel to carry as much sail as will enable her to get out to sea. In February, March, and April, there is much fog at the entrance of the Mississippi. From December to March there are frequently strong northerly winds: and if these winds veer to East or South of East, the weather becomes dark, cloudy, or foggy.

Coast from the Bay of San Bernardo to Tampico.—Between the Bay of San Bernardo and Tampico winds from S.E. continue from April till August; during the other months of the year strong winds from East and E.S.E. are found on that coast, lasting two or three days before blowing from North. During the fine season, the land breezes prevail regularly from eleven or twelve at night to nine or ten in the morning.

Tampico to Vera Cruz.—On the coast from Tampico to Vera Cruz, from April to July, the winds during the day blow from East, veering to E.S.E.; during the night they veer to South and S.W.; that is, off the land. If the land breeze, on the contrary, shifts to N.W., accompanied by a little rain, the next day the wind generally comes from North of N.N.E. or N.E., especially in August and September. The land winds are termed *Vientos de cabeza* (head winds) or *Vendavales*. These winds are generally light; they do not reach further than twenty or thirty leagues from the coast, at which distance they blow from East or E.S.E.

Vera Cruz.—At Vera Cruz the winter season commences towards the middle of May, and terminates towards the end of July, when there are frequent interruptions in the Trade winds, much fog, and stormy weather. From November to February the northerly winds blow very strong and storms are heavy.

The most violent winds are from East, but do not last long. Northerly winds prevail from September till March, but they generally fall at sunset, blowing strongest from nine o'clock in the morning till three in the afternoon. This is not the case if the wind only gets up in the afternoon or evening, in which case it continues to blow during the night, gradually increasing in force. At night, and after midnight, the wind changes, and shifts to N.W., blowing from the land. In this case if towards morning it veers to S.W., the North wind will not last, and the sea breeze will follow at the usual time, about nine or ten in the morning; but if this does not take place towards sunrise, or at latest at the beginning of tide, the North wind will again blow with as much force as on the preceding day; it is then called the North tide wind. The North wind often terminates by shifting to East, a guarantee of fine weather. If in the afternoon it veers to N.E., the sky will be cloudy the next morning; when the land breeze has come from South to West during the night a sea breeze may be expected in the evening.

The weather then continues fine during five or six days; the longest period of fair weather with northerly winds. In case of the winds backing from N.E. to N.N.E. and North, the weather is uncertain.* An attention to these peculiarities of the winds is important as affecting the approaches to the coast of Vera Cruz.

Coast of Yucatan from Vera Cruz to Point Arena.—On the coast of Yucatan, from Vera Cruz to Arenas, we find, during the dry season, alternate land and sea breezes. The sea breeze comes from North, the land breeze from South, from seven or eight o'clock in the evening till eight or nine in the morning. The dry season lasts from September till April or May. The rainy season follows, and continues till September; it is announced by tornadoes and violent storms, which become more frequent in May and June. The great rains fall in July and August, being then continuous and very heavy. In this season there are sometimes strong winds from E.S.E., lasting three or four days.

Winds from North to N.E. begin in October; they are very strong in December and January, and gradually fail toward March; in general they are fresh and dry, and stronger than the common breeze.

*Bernardo de Orta: *Derrotero de las Antillas.*

Coast from Point Arenas to Cape Catoche.—On that part of the coast comprised between Point Arenas and Cape Catoche, the seasons are nearly the same as the foregoing, only the general winds are from N.E., interrupted by strong North winds. In April tornadoes occur from N.E. to S.E. The squally weather lasts till September, during which sea breezes set in from N.N.W. to N.W. These breezes rise at eleven o'clock in the morning and during the night veer to East and E.S.E., and afterwards to S.E.; which last may therefore be regarded as land breezes.

It has been observed here, that the stronger the wind is from N.N.W. to N.W. the more violent are the tornadoes. On this part of the coast it has also been remarked that the rainy season is shorter than on the neighbouring coast westward.

Antilles.—The N.E. Trade wind prevails particularly over that portion of sea called the Caribbean Sea. When approaching the shores of these isles, however, disturbances are found in those winds. Thus, on the shores of the Great Antilles, Cuba, Jamaica, St. Domingo, and Porto Rico, the sea breeze blows regularly during the day, and the land breeze during the night. The land breezes are fresher than those observed near the coast, and are favourable for making passages from West to East in this sea.

In the Lesser Antilles the land breeze is not met with, or if it should be it is at so short a distance from the shore as to be useless in navigation. In these islands two seasons are observed,—the dry and the rainy. Their periods vary in the different islands;

but it may be stated generally, that the first lasts from October to June, and the second from June to October. During the dry season the N.E. Trade wind blows regularly and fresh with a clear sky. From June to October (the winter season) tornadoes and severe hurricanes are experienced, between the 15th of July and the 15th of October. In the Antilles the hurricanes blow from the West. This is a necessary consequence of the focus of the hurricane passing to the northward of them, as it usually does.

Hurricanes rarely penetrate into the Gulf of Mexico; some, however, have crossed the gulf, and continued onward beyond Vera Cruz. Amongst others, those of the 18th of August, 1810, and June 23rd, 1831.

We quote the following statement of the course of the hurricanes in the Atlantic from a little pocket treatise on hurricanes. "In the Atlantic Ocean, it is shown by Redfield that their average place of commencement is in the latitude of 15° N., and longitude 55° W., or about N.E. from the island of Trinidad. From thence they pursue a W.N.W. course, until arriving near the coast of Florida they follow the course of the Gulf Stream to the N.E., sweeping past the coast of the United States, and continuing far beyond the eastern limits of Newfoundland. Some, originating South of those, have maintained their western course beyond the Gulf of Mexico; and others, again, North of them, have assumed their N.E. course, passing between Bermuda and the American coast. But the North Atlantic hurricane mostly commences

N.E. of Trinidad, within the parallels of 10° and 20° N. and between 50° and 60° West longitude." *

Calms and Storms.—Under the lee of the high lands which form the greater part of the Antilles, calm is experienced, interrupted by violent and very dangerous squalls, coming down from the declivities of the mountains; and it is only at two or three leagues off at sea that the regular breeze is again found. These tricks of the wind announce their approach by a shrill whistling, and sometimes by an agitation of the surface of the sea. They must not be trusted in sailing by the wind from the islands, and great care is necessary in looking to the sails. Vessels have been dismasted by these breezes, and many have been capsized even at the entrance of the bay where they had intended to anchor. During winter strong tide rips are found in most of the bays of the Antilles, generally after calms or light airs.

Cuba.—At Cuba the rainy season is from June to September, and the N.E. Trade wind blows over the whole island from March to October. During the other months it takes frequently a northerly direction, changing to N.W.: it is then sometimes very strong. In the fine season, the sea breeze is regular on the North coast; it commences towards eleven o'clock or at noon, and towards evening gives place to the land breeze. It is found, however, that the Trade wind prevails on this coast of the island, and that winds from South to East frequently prevail in the morning

* *Storm Compass; or, Seaman's Hurricane Companion, by A. B. Becher, Captain, R.N.*, p. 5. Potter, 31, Poultry, London.

and shift from E.N.E. to N.E. towards evening. At Havana the sea breeze generally sets in about ten o'clock in the morning.

On the South coast there are alternate land and sea breezes, the land wind commencing shortly after sunset.

The Bahama Isles.—The following observations of one year were made at Nassau, in the isle of Providence:—

Months.	Winds.	Remarks on the Weather.
January ..	S., N.E., N.N.E.	Strong breezes and cloudy.
February ..	N.E., S.E., N.E.	Moderate and variable.
March	N.E., S.E., N.E., N.	Clear, but breezy.
April	E., N.E., S.E., N.W.	Clear, a little rain.
May	Variable.	Moderate, showery.
June	Ditto.	Clear and dry.
July	S.E., E., S., N.E.	Light and clear.
August	N.E., E., N., W., S.	Squalls, with rain.
September.	Ditto.	Clear, rain, and fog.
October ..	E., N.E., N.W.	Light, rain, and squalls.
November..	S., S.W., W., N.W.	Moderate and squally.
December..	S., S.W., N.W.	Variable, light, clear.

Jamaica.—In the island of Jamaica the alternate land and sea breezes are well established during the fine season; the former extend four leagues from the coast and cease towards four in the morning. The following are observations made on the winds of this island:—

Months.	Winds.	Remarks on the Weather.
January ..	N. and S.E.	Fine, small rain; strong winds from N.
February ..	Ditto.	Fine and dry; strong sea breezes.
March	Ditto.	Ditto.
April......	Ditto.	Very dry; breezes moderate.
May	Ditto.	Fine; some showers.
June	Ditto.	Generally fine; heavy rain.
July	Ditto.	Much rain; fine by intervals.
August	S.S.W.	Some heavy rains.
September..	S.S.W. and S.E.	Fine mornings; rain in the afternoon.
October ..	Ditto.	Heavy rain by intervals; generally fine.
November..	Ditto.	Ditto.
December..	Ditto.	A little rain; generally fine.

On all the coast of this island alternate land and sea breezes are found, and their directions vary according to that of the coasts. The sea breeze commences about eight or nine a.m., increases till noon,—sometimes till four p.m., and afterwards diminishes, to give place to the land breeze, which ceases towards four or six o'clock in the morning.

Porto Rico.—At Porto Rico rain falls from June to August. The Trade winds blow from N.E. The sea breeze commences at eight in the morning and lasts till four in the afternoon, when it is followed by the land breeze.

St. Domingo.—The winds in the island of Hayti or St. Domingo vary on different parts of its shores. The winter season lasts from the end of April till November. During this season squalls of wind and storms are frequent; and strong winds from S.E. are found in the bay of Gonaives and in the channel of St. Mark. In November, December, January, and February, northerly winds, changing to N.W., blow violently, principally on the North coast of the island. On the South coast, in June, July, and August, there are frequent storms, with the wind, from South, blowing violently. On the shores of this island, the land wind, which is generally very light when it does blow, is not to be depended on.

Lesser Antilles.—The following observations made at Trinidad and Dominica will give a general idea of the winds met with in the Lesser Antilles. The first table is for the isle of Trinidad :—

Months.	Winds.	Remarks on the Weather.
January ...	E., E.N.E., E.S.E.	Cloudy, rain.
February ...	E. and E.N.E.	Cloudy, heavy dew.
March	Ditto.	Fine, dry.
April.........	E.N.E.	Fresh breezes.
May	S.E. and E.N.E.	Strong winds, thunder.
June	E.N.E. and E.S.E.	Rainy, breezes.
July	E.N.E.	Tempests, rain, and storms.
August......	E.S.E.	Heavy gusts of wind, rain, and storms.
September..	Ditto.	Heavy rain, storms.
October	Ditto.	Strong breezes.
November..	E. and E.N.E.	Fine and warm occasionally.
December...	Ditto.	Cold.

The following table is for the island of Dominica :—

Months.	Winds.	Remarks on the Weather.
January ...	E.N.E. and N.	Cloudy.
February ...	E.N.E. and S.E.	Cold.
March	N.E. to S.E.	Fine, sometimes cloudy.
April.........	E.N.E., S.E., S.	Fine, moderate breezes.
May	N.E. to S.E. and E.	Calm, weather clear.
June	S.E., E. to N.E.	Calm, fog, and rain.
July	Ditto.	Calm, nights cold.
August......	S.E. and N.E.	Calm, nights cold, storms and gusts.
September..	S. and S.E.	Generally fine, rain at intervals.
October	N.E. to S.E.	Cloudy and fine alternately.
November..	Ditto.	Fine and dry.
December...	Ditto.	Fine, dry, and cold.

East Coast of Yucatan, Vera Paz, Honduras, and Mosquito.—On the eastern coast of Yucatan, and of Vera Paz, Hondúras, and Mosquito, which form the western coast of the Caribbean Sea, the N.E. Trade wind prevails in February, March, April, and May, but is sometimes interrupted (principally during the two first months) by northerly winds. In June, July, and August, the winds on these coasts vary from East to West by the South, attended by squalls and calms. In October, November, December, and January, the winds are from South to North, changing by the West, with squalls from W.S.W. to W.N.W., shifting to the North.

On the coast between Cape Gracias a Dios and Cape La Vela the winds are very changeable. From March to November they blow from N.E. to East but are often interrupted by tornadoes in May, June, and July. Between the months of October and March, particularly in December and January, the wind occasionally comes from West; it is not strong, but sometimes lasts during seven or eight days, and is then followed by N.E. winds.

While the westerly wind is strong on this coast, lasting for some days, the Trade wind from East nevertheless is blowing out at sea as at other times. It is met with at a distance of eight or ten leagues from Cape La Vela at the same time that the westerly winds are blowing on the coast near this cape.

Porto Bello.—At Porto Bello, and between this point and Cartagena, the wind is N.E. from the 15th of November till the 15th of May. At the end of May it veers to S.W. and W.S.W., and reaches as far as lat. 12° N. These winds from S.W. and W.S.W., which are sometimes very violent, bring rain. At twenty leagues seaward from Porto Bello the wind blows from South in the interior of the gulf, veering to N.E.; the South winds generally extend eight or nine leagues from the coast. The winds from S.W. and W.S.W. are termed *vendavales*.

Cartagena.—At Cartagena during the fine season, from the middle of December till the end of April, the wind is generally from N.E. From May till November (the winter season) rainy and stormy weather prevails. During the fine season N.E. winds become settled towards the 15th of November. In the rainy season S.W. and W.S.W. winds extend as far as lat. 12° N.; beyond which the wind takes a N.E. direction. In November and December there are strong breezes, with much rain. During the winter season tornadoes are frequent on the coast.

Coasts of Caracas and Cumana.—The Trade winds take their usual course on the coasts of Caracas and Cumana as far as Cape La Vela; but from this cape to the point of St. Blaize their direction varies from N.E. to N.N.E. During the months of March, April, May, and June, they are more regular, blowing with great violence from E.N.E. These strong breezes extend from the middle of the channel to within two or three leagues of the land, and diminish in force as they near it. On these two coasts, and even as far as the Gulf of Nicaragua, the rainy westerly winds, to which we have already alluded, called *vendavales*, are found from July to December, and sometimes till January.

CHAPTER VII.

Guiana Coast—Brazil Coast—Rio Janeiro—River Plate—Pamperos—Patagonia—Terra del Fuego —Falkland Islands—Azores—Bermuda.

Coast of Guiana.—On the coast of Guiana the Trade wind only is found. From January to March it is from N.N.E. to E.N.E. In April, May, and June, there are variable winds and calms. Afterwards the Trade veers to E.S.E. and S.E., blowing from S.E. principally between June and December. The dry season is from January to June, and the rainy season is attended by continual storms.

The following table shows the state of the winds and weather at Demerara:—

Months.	Winds.	Remarks on the Weather.
January ..	East.	Cold, fresh breezes.
February ..	N.E.	Thick clouds, with tempests, stormy.
March	E.N.E.	Clouds, very heavy showers.
April......	East.	Heat, no rain.
May	N.E.	Thick clouds, frequent lightning, rain.
June......	South and Variable.	Hot, and rain at intervals.
July	East and South.	Hot, and very heavy.
August....	South.	Hot, rain at intervals.
September..	South and East.	Heat, thunder and lightning.
October....	Variable.	Light breezes, showers.
November..	North and East.	Ditto.
December..	N.N.E.	Heavy rain, breezes cold.

On the coasts of French Guiana the winter season begins in November and ends in July; the dry season lasts from July to November. Winds from E.N.E. blow during the first period; those from E.S.E. during the second. The rainy season is from December to February, and sometimes till March; it even begins sometimes sooner,—about the 15th of November. In March and April there is an interval of three weeks or a month during which time the rains cease. This period in French Guiana is termed the March summer. The rain begins again towards the middle of April, and terminates in the middle of July. From November to March the winds are from N.N.E. to N.E.; during March and April they change from East to South; from May to June they return to N.E., calms then are rare, and there is no land wind. It is observed at Guiana that the dry winds are from East to South.

North Coast of Brazil.—On the North coast of Brazil, as far as Cape St. Roque, the Trade winds blow from N.E. to S.E. From July to December those from S.E. to East prevail; from December to July those from N.E. to East. The change in these periodical winds occurs in June, and during this month calms are frequently met with in the vicinity of the coast, but they are subject to interruption by squalls of wind and rain. The heaviest squalls are with the wind from East to N.E. At a short distance from this coast a land wind is often found during the night and morning, varying from S.S.E. to South, and ceasing towards eight or nine a.m.

East Coast of Brazil.—On the East coast of Brazil the winds are periodical. From September to March they blow from E.N.E. to N.E.; from March to September from S.S.E. to E.S.E. These winds do not extend more than forty or fifty leagues out to sea. Beyond this limit the Trade wind is found, which generally blows between S.E. and East. On this limit, however, variable winds are met between S.S.W. and S.E., with rain and storms. On the North part of this coast rain is frequent, as well as variable winds in March and September,—the times when the change of winds takes place,—accompanied by heavy squally weather.

Bahia de Todos los Santos.—At Bahia the wind is E.N.E. from September till April. From April till August it is from South, changing from S.E. to S.S.W. In April it begins shifting to South and S.S.W. It is in greatest force during May, June, July, and August, and in these months is from S.E., varying to South and S.S.W. The seasons change in April and September. The wet season at Bahia begins in April, the same as on the coast of Brazil. The fine weather returns in September.

Rio Janeiro.—At Rio Janeiro, the sea breeze, which comes from East, begins at eleven a.m., but only reaches the roadstead and town towards one or two p.m., although the latter is only three leagues from the entrance of the bay. The sea breeze lasts till sunset. The land breeze commences towards evening and lasts till morning, its duration and force depending on the season of the year.

River La Plata.—The winds in the River La Plata and at the mouth of it follow the course of the seasons, but the form of its shores and their proximity exercise so great an influence on their force and direction that they are rarely the same as in the interior of the river. Thus sometimes a violent wind is blowing at Buenos Ayres which is not felt on the shore immediately opposite.

Almost all the pilots attribute great influence to the phases of the moon, and agree that it is difficult to foretell the weather correctly, the changes of the atmosphere being so sudden as to defy all their predictions. Storms gather and come down so rapidly that it is necessary to be always on guard against them. Instances of violent storms, called *pamperos*, are cited as coming suddenly when the weather was fine and clear, and announced only by a whirlwind; these, however, come only with a N.W. or westerly wind.

In this country the wind from S.W. is termed the *pampero*, coming as it does from the *pampas* or plains. It is generally introduced by thick black clouds, which appear to roll hurriedly over each other; at other times by a large dark arch which invades the whole sky from West to East. The horizon quickly clears towards the S.W., and it is then that the *pampero* bursts forth with indescribable fury. It is frequently accompanied by thunder, lightning, and rain; the coldness of the temperature is quite uncomfortable. The sky soon, however, becomes clear and the weather fine, and continues so during the rest of the *pampero*.

When the wind ceases it almost always veers to South and S.E. Before the *pampero* bursts forth the barometer is very low; the mercury begins rising towards the end of the squalls, when the wind shifts to South.

In the River La Plata, and also at sea in the same parallel, the winds are very changeable; during the fine season, from September to March, the prevailing wind out at sea is from N.E.; the horizon is charged with vapour, and the sky filled with clouds of indefinite forms. On nearing the river the wind veers to East, sometimes to S.E., very fresh, with rain and cloudy weather.

In the interior of the river, during this season, the wind from S.E. blows regularly in the afternoon; at night it falls and shifts to North: this wind is called a *virazon:* when it falls, and the wind from North to N.W. continues, a storm from S.W. (*pampero*) may be expected, more or less violent according to the *virazon.* We repeat, that great precautions are necessary against these storms, or they may prove fatal to those who are not prepared to meet them.

About the times of full and change of the moon, strong breezes are found from S.E., with rain; sometimes also the wind blows from North, not so strong as that from S.E., and the temperature is higher.

The pilots say that the S.E. wind blows when the moon has South declination, and the North wind when she has North declination. In these cases the North wind generally shifts to N.E. in dry weather; if accompanied by rain or heavy dew it veers to N.W. It often becomes violent, blows in squalls from this direction, and ends by shifting to S.W., blowing strongly; with this wind the sea rises suddenly, and subsides as soon as it ceases.

From March to September the general winds at the entrance of the La Plata are from West to S.W. Ascending the river they are more frequently northward instead of southward of West.

The winter season is preferable to that of summer in the roadstead of Buenos Ayres; for the wind being generally from S.W. to N.W. the river is smooth and communication thereby facilitated.

In the months of July, August, and September, there is frequently a thick fog from the mouth of the river to the shore of Ortiz; further up this is not so frequent.

The inhabitants of La Plata attribute these prejudicial influences to the North wind: it is in fact very hot, and while it blows the air is charged with electricity; thus the wind from this quarter almost always terminates in a storm, during which it shifts to S.W. and restores the equilibrium.

Sometimes the *pamperos* extend out to sea, and pass the latitude of the island of St. Catherine. When it is clear they last longer than when the clouds are charged. What has been said respecting the winds of La Plata at sea, at its mouth, and in the interior, is what takes place in a general way; but the contrary must not occasion surprise, for the wind is so variable that neither its duration nor direction can be depended on with certainty: frequently during consecutive years at the same seasons the winds are widely different.

East Coast of Patagonia.—Ships leaving the Atlantic and bound for any port in the Pacific, will derive 'advantage from keeping within at least a hundred miles from the East coast of Patagonia, as much to avoid the heavy sea caused by the westerly breezes which predominate, and are stronger according to the distance from shore, as to profit by the variableness of the westerly wind. Near the coast, from April to September, when the sun has North declination, the wind is more from W.N.W. and N.N.W. than from any other quarter. Easterly winds are very rare, but when they do take place, as they come obliquely to the coast, there is no danger in keeping in shore.

During the opposite season, when the sun has South declination, the wind is principally from the southward of West, and sometimes very strong; but as the coast is to windward the sea falls with the wind. Although during this season the wind may not be fair, yet as it is rarely steady, and often varies six or eight points, backwards or forwards, in a few hours; advantage may be taken of this circumstance by keeping near the shore.

Terra del Fuego.—Fogs are very rare on the coast of Terra del Fuego: but dark and rainy weather, accompanied by violent winds, is generally experienced there. The sun appears but seldom, and even in fine weather the sky is dull and cloudy, and the atmosphere very seldom clear.

Different winds succeed each other at short intervals, and last several days; sometimes the weather is fine for the space of a fortnight; but this happens very rarely.

The equinoctial months are the worst of the whole year about Terra del Fuego and Cape Horn. The winds are then strong, but may not always be expected on the exact day of the equinox.

The months of August, September, October, and November, are also generally worse than the others. During these months westerly winds prevail, as well as snow, rain, and intense cold. December, January, and February, are the hottest months. The days are then long, and the weather sometimes fine. But in these months westerly winds prevail, sometimes very strong, and accompanied by much rain; for even the summer in these latitudes only possesses the advantage of longer days and a less rigorous temperature.

March is subject to storms, and is perhaps the worst month in the year, on account of the sudden squalls which then take place. It is, however, not so rainy as the summer months.

In April, May, and June, fine weather is general, and although the days shorten at this time, the weather resembles that of summer more than at any other period of the year. Bad weather is nevertheless found during these months; but the easterly winds, which are frequent, bring with them some fine days.

Passage from the Atlantic to the Pacific.—June and July are much alike, only in July the easterly winds are more frequent. The shortness of the days and the extreme cold renders these months very unpleasant, although they are perhaps the most favourable for sailing from the Atlantic to the Pacific Ocean, because the wind so frequently blows from the East.

On the contrary, the summer months, namely, December and January, are the best for passing from the Pacific to the Atlantic Ocean, though this passage is so short and easy that it may be attempted at all times.

In these regions thunder and lightning are little known. Violent storms are announced by heavy clouds coming from South and S.W.; they are accompanied sometimes by snow and hail of large dimensions, which render them still more formidable.

Westerly winds prevail during a great part of the year in these parts, and about Cape Horn. The easterly winds only blow during the winter months now and then; they are, however, violent during this season, and are very rare during summer.

The easterly winds are generally accompanied by fine weather; when they begin blowing they gradually increase in strength. The weather then changes, and the breeze perhaps again becomes somewhat fresher; they often obtain such a force as to require three reefs in the topsails; then they gradually fall or shift to another quarter.

The North winds commence by blowing moderately, but the weather is more gloomy and cloudy than with an easterly wind, and a little rain generally falls. In proportion as the wind freshens, it veers westward and increases in force, blowing between North and

N.W. The sky then is very cloudy and dark, and rain falls abundantly. From N.W. it blows hard, and when its force is expended (which it is in about twelve or fifteen hours), or even while it blows hard from this quarter, the breeze suddenly shifts to S.W., and blows more violently than before. The wind disperses the clouds, and in a few hours the weather is perfectly clear; nevertheless, at times the squalls are very severe. The wind continues several days in the S.W. quarter, generally blowing very fresh; then it moderates a little, and, after two or three days, the weather becomes fine.

The North winds generally blow during summer, and it is a fact established from observation that the shifting of the wind from North to South takes place by the West during this season—one which would little deserve its name were not the days longer and the atmosphere warmer. The winds and rain are much more violent during the long than during the short days.

It should not be forgotten that bad weather never comes suddenly from East, and that a S.W. or South wind never shifts quickly to North. On the contrary, winds from South and S.W. come on suddenly and with violence.

South winds and storms from S.W. are preceded and announced by thick masses of large white clouds rising in these parts, the borders of which are clearly defined, and which appear round and solid.

The North winds are preceded and accompanied by very low clouds; the sky is overcast. The sun can scarcely penetrate them and assumes a reddish aspect.

Some hours, and even a whole day, before a North or N.W. wind the altitude of the sun cannot be taken, although it is visible, because the misty atmosphere prevents its disc from being distinctly seen.

Sometimes, but rarely, with a slight breeze, varying from N.N.W. to N.N.E., there are a few days of fine weather. South breezes and rain generally follow. The most common weather in these regions is a cloudy sky with a fresh breeze, varying from N.W. to S.W.

Falkland Isles.—It would be difficult to find a region more exposed to storms in summer and winter than that of the Falkland Islands.

The winds there are very variable, rarely falling while the sun is above the horizon, and sometimes very violent, even in summer. A day of calm is an extraordinary fact at the Falkland Isles. Generally it blows less during the night than during the day; but, both by day and night, at all times of the year, they are exposed to sudden and violent storms and squalls of wind, though these do not usually last more than a few hours.

The prevailing wind is westerly. It generally begins from N.W., shifting to S.W. by the West; and when the N.W. wind is attended by rain it quickly passes to S.W. and blows strong from that quarter.

The North winds produce cloudy weather, and when they are light are accompanied by thick fog. It is also observed that they usually blow about the times of the moon's quartering. The winds from N.E. and North produce very gloomy weather, with much rain. They are sometimes strong and veer to N.N.W., but most frequently to West. S.E. winds also bring rain. They are rather frequent and blow strong, and in proportion as they strengthen they veer to the southward.

During winter the principal winds are from N.W., and in summer from S.W. Although sometimes fogs attend the wind from East and North, they do not often last for a day.

The squalls of wind from the South, from S.W., and S.E., are more violent and sudden than those from any other direction. East winds are seldom strong, and last only a short time. They generally produce fair weather and may be expected more during April, May, June, and July, than at any other time of the year. Intervals of fine weather are very scarce in the course of the year when the wind is varying between E.S.E. and E.N.E.

Thunder and lightning are very rare, and with the latter easterly winds may be expected. If lightning appears in the S.E., and the barometer is low, a heavy breeze of wind from that quarter will most likely follow.

These breezes from S.E. and South last longer than those from West, at least mostly so, and they cause a heavy surf on the South coasts of these islands. In winter the wind is generally not so strong as in summer, and during winter the weather, though colder, is drier and more settled.

At Stanley, the principal port of these islands, ships can at all times be refitted, and can obtain any stores of which they may be in need.

All important changes are foretold by the barometer, and provided the changes of the mercury are understood by those who consult them, the necessary precautions can always be taken in time.

Azores.—From a register kept during ten years by Mr. T. C. Hunt, while British Consul at St. Michael, it appears that the Azores seldom experience more than a week of calm days throughout the year. The prevailing winds are N.E. and N.W.: the former more in the summer than in the winter months: the S.W. are less frequent, and the S.E. still less; those from the cardinal points being but few. The boisterous character of the climate of these islands is proverbial, but they are in a boisterous latitude.

At Ponta Delgada, Island of St. Michael's, an artificial harbour has been constructed, where vessels even of large size can remain in safety. There are ample facilities for repairs, and supplies of all kinds are obtainable.

There is also a floating dock, capable of receiving vessels not drawing more than 14 feet.

Bermuda.—The prevailing winds in winter are from N.W. to S.W. Violent tempests and squalls occur during the winter months. In the summer the winds are light and variable.

Maury says, taking the Atlantic Ocean, North and South, as an index of what takes place in other waters (seas), the abstract logs therein show that for every gale of wind that seamen encounter on the equatorial side of these two parallels of 30° North and South, they encounter 10·4 on the polar side; and that for every fog on the equatorial they encounter 83 on the polar side. It appears from these, however, that both the most stormy and foggy latitudes in the North Atlantic are between the parallels of 45° and 50°; that in the South Atlantic the most stormy latitudes are between the parallels of 55° and 60°, the most foggy between 50° and 55°. The Azores, however, which are between 36° and 40°, are more remarkable for strong winds than thick fogs.

The following observation made on the winds in the neighbourhood of Cape Finisterre may be of service to the navigator.

It may be said that there are but two prevailing winds on the North and West coast of Spain, the N.E. in summer, and in winter the S.W. The N.E. wind in summer brings clear weather, lasting for above a fortnight, and only interrupted by S.W. or westerly winds of short duration. But a N.E. wind in winter will bring thick cloudy weather and rain as well as in summer if blowing a gale.

The S.W. winds, called *vendavales*, are frequently attended with bad weather. Westerly and N.W. winds clear the sky, but southerly winds bring dark rainy weather.

Such are the general observations on the winds in the different parts of the basin of the Atlantic. We shall now proceed to consider the currents of this sea.

CHAPTER VIII.

Currents of the Atlantic—Atlantic Equatorial Current—Guiana and Counter Equatorial Current—The Westerly Drift—Caribbean Sea and Gulf of Mexico—Gulf Stream—Arctic Current—Rennel Current—Portugal Current—Guinea Current—Brazil Current—Currents of the Southern Capes—South Atlantic Polar Current.

The currents of the Atlantic are of two kinds: one occasioned by tides, and found only at short distances from the coast; the other arising from various causes; but they are almost constant in their direction, and deviate only near those coasts which impede their progress.

These last, called general currents, are divided into cold and warm currents, according to the waters of which they are composed. The result of all observations on currents may be thus expressed:—Cold currents flow from the poles towards the equator on the western coasts of continents. Currents setting from East to West flow along the equator; warm currents flowing from the equator towards the poles pass along the eastern shores of great continents. Thus we find a cold current setting from North to South on the western coasts of Europe and the N.W. coast of Africa: a cold current from South to North on the S.W. coast of the same continent. But, on the contrary, on the coast of Brazil a warm current is found flowing from North to South: then a warm current, which after having circulated through the Gulf of Mexico leaves it by the Bahamas, and flows along the coast of the United States, being known by the name of the Gulf Stream.

Such are the general currents of that vast basin, called the Atlantic Ocean, formed by an immense longitudinal valley, separating the European and African continents from those of America.

Philosophers differ as to the originating causes of these general currents. Some attribute them to the action of the Trade winds; while the greater number admit that, like the winds, they are produced by the sun's heat, and by the rotatory motion of the earth. Thus, they say, in consequence of this movement, and the passage of the polar waters towards the equator, a current, directed from East to West, must be formed at the equator, similar to that which takes place in the atmosphere and is produced by the same cause.

Now, a constant current must necessarily produce a drain of the waters adjacent to one of its extremes, say the eastern, and on the contrary a lateral displacement at the opposite one, the western; or, in other words, admit a flow of the polar waters towards the equator on the western coast of the great equatorial continents, then necessarily a flow towards the poles in the eastern sides of the continents must ensue. We may further observe that the equatorial waters as they flow onwards for the poles, on account of the greater velocity of rotation at the equator, as well as on account of the flow of the polar waters toward the equator, should follow a certain direction easterly from the West, like the Gulf Stream in the North Atlantic and the current of the South Atlantic flowing from the coast of Brazil towards the Cape of Good Hope.

Equatorial, Polar, and Tropical Currents.—We call the Equatorial current that which flows from East to West at the equator. We shall distinguish by the name of *polar currents* those flowing from the poles towards the equator on the western coasts of the continents; and by the name of *tropical currents* those flowing from the equator towards the poles on the eastern coasts of the continents. The velocity of these currents varies in different parts of their courses; the greatest that has been observed is from 60 to 120 miles in twenty-four hours. Their general temperature is higher or lower than that of the sea through which they pass, according to that of the climate where they originate. We shall now consider the direction and limits of the Atlantic currents, showing their mean velocities and temperatures; and first those of the Equatorial current.

Equatorial Current.—The Equatorial current commences off the West coast of Africa in about 5° 30′ E. of Greenwich. It passes by the Isle of Anno Bom and continues westward parallel to the equator between 1° or 1° 30′ N. lat. and 5° to 8° S. It soon extends itself northward, and although it hardly passes North of 1° 30′, it extends abreast of Cape Palmas as far as 8° S. lat. For the space of about 1,500 miles, nearly as far as 20° or 23° W. in lat. 1° to 3° North of the equator it runs by the side of another current taking the opposite direction, from West to East, called the Guinea current. This portion of the sea then presents the remarkable phenomena of two currents adjacent to each other running with great velocity in opposite directions, and having a difference of temperature of about seven degrees; so that imagining a vessel to be in either of these currents sailing eastward in the Gulf of Guinea, her progress would be accelerated or retarded forty or fifty miles a day, that being the rapidity of the two currents in this part. We shall hereafter return to this important fact. In October and November the line of separation is found on the 20th meridian in 5° N.—in March and April about 2° 30′ N.; and on the 5th meridian it is generally in 2° N.

Advancing westward in a stream extending from 2° N. to nearly 10° S. the Equatorial current in 20° W. commences to change its course, the northern part trending slightly to the North, and the southern portion altering its course more rapidly towards the South. When about 300 miles from Cape St. Roque it divides into two distinct branches, the largest, which might be called the main stream, passing to the N.W. along the coast of Guiana until it reaches the Antilles, this branch is known by the name of the Guiana current: the southern portion running parallel to the coast of South America and extending far out to sea, forming the Brazil current.

The Equatorial Current.—Extent.—The length of the Equatorial current from the coast of Africa to Cape St. Roque is 2,500 miles, and to the Antilles

4,000 miles. Its breadth abreast of Cape Palmas 600 miles; and it runs for 2,000 miles before it finally divides.

Velocity.—This current has most velocity in summer and least in winter. Near the equator, between the meridians of 5° E. and 8° W., its mean rate is from 25 to 30 miles a day. Between 8° and 14° W. long., towards the end of June, and the beginning of July, it varies from 30 to 75 miles. Between 14° and 21° W. long., from 20 to 79; its mean velocity may then be estimated at 40 miles in twenty-four hours.

The Meteorological Department of the Board of Trade, from an analysis of ships' registers, obtained the following information respecting the set and force of this current in the neighbourhood of the Rocas:—

4 Vessels,	set West,	48 to 24	miles	a day.
7 ,,	do.	20 to 10	,,	,,
4 ,,	W.N.W.	51 to 30	,,	,,
4 ,,	do.	29 to 21	,,	,,
3 ,,	W.S.W.	48 to 30	,,	,,
2 ,,	do.	20 to 10	,,	,,
1 ,,	S.W.	40	,,	,,

The current was found strongest in June, July, August, and November.

The following table, showing the average daily set in miles, has been compiled from the Admiralty Current Charts:—

	40° W. to 30° W.	to 20° W.	to 10° W.	to 0	to 5° E.
N. of Equator	25	39	47	35	20
Equator to 5° S.	28*	31	35	31	24
5° S. to 10° S.	20	26	24	14	14

* Near Cape San Roque the set to the N.W. amounts to 60 miles.

The *Scotia*, when engaged repairing a submarine telegraph cable in latitude 2° N. and longitude 30° 40′ W., during seventeen days in November and December, 1883, experienced a current running to the westward at the rate of about 1½ knots.

Temperature.—The mean temperature of its waters is 73°; from June to September, even as far as 20° W., it is some 10° lower than the Guinea current.

The Guiana Current.—The Guiana current, which is a continuation of the Equatorial current, runs along the low coast of Guiana towards the island of Trinidad. About the equator it is crossed by the waters of the Amazon, a river which, receiving an immense volume of water from tributaries, forms a cross-current to it, producing considerable overfalls. This, however, owing to the impetuosity of the fresh water, does not influence its direction. The river waters and those of the Guiana current do not intermingle with each other; for after crossing that current the river water is recognised at 300 miles from its mouth.

A little South of Trinidad the River Orinoco discharges a considerable quantity of water into the Guiana current. From the nearly similar directions in which they run the waters easily combine with each other, and the rapidity of the current is thus considerably augmented. It then enters the sea of the Antilles by the strait formed on one side by the Island of Trinidad and on the other by that of Martinique; in which space are the islands of St. Vincent, St. Lucia, Grenada, Barbados, and Tobago.

Velocity of the Guiana Current.—The Guiana

current varies in strength from 15 to 70 miles a day. It has been sometimes found to be four miles an hour, while near the coast it gradually diminishes to less than half a mile an hour.

Temperature.—The temperature of the waters of this current has been estimated at 80°; that of the waters of the River Amazon very near the line of demarcation is also 80°. The line of separation between the waters of the Amazon and those of this current is N.W. ½ N., and the two waters are as distinct from each other as two separate fluids.

Counter Equatorial Current.—Modern investigations have quite confirmed the existence of this current setting to the eastward at certain periods, between the northern limits of the Equatorial current and latitude 10° N. In May and June it is found in about 30° W., in July and August it reaches as far as 53° W., in September and October drawing East again to 40° W., in November to 30° W., it then merges into the Guinea current.

The velocity is very variable, from 60 miles a day in 45° W. to 15 miles in 35° W.

The knowledge of the existence of this current is of great importance to the navigator.

We append the following extract from the *Nautical Magazine* relative to this counter-current near the Equator, being remarks made by Lieutenant de Brito Capello, of the Portuguese Royal Navy, suggested by a discussion on the winds of the Gulf of Guinea. He says: "I will call your attention to the interesting subject which these charts make very evident. I allude to the origin of the Guinea current. Kerhalet and other authors who notice this current make it depend entirely on the Polar current of the coast of Africa, which, they say, to the southward of Cape Verd Islands turns to the S.E., following the coast, and at Cape Palmas turns East and E.N.E., thus constituting the Guinea current.

"I think that the origin of the Guinea current is not due to that; at least, in the months of July, August, and September, when this current shows itself with its greatest force, an easterly current is observed from 35° or 40° W. of Greenwich. This mass of water comes between the parallels of 5° and 10° N., running on the coast between the Bijoogas and Cape Palmas, and so far from forming a junction with the Polar current, it is this which keeps it to the southward, obliging it to take its S.E. course.

"At the period when the Guinea current is comparatively weak, it is very true that the Polar current reinforces the Guinea current along the coast; but nevertheless, the charts show a kind of course independent of it, situated at the apex of the triangular space of calms, where the wind, very weak, changes its direction from S.E. to S.W., and from N.E. to N.W.

"May not the atmospheric pressure have some reference to this source of the Guinea current? In the zone of the calms the barometric pressure is five or seven-tenths less than in the adjacent parts;—might not this diminished pressure be the cause of an elevation of the waters nearly thirteen times more, as has been already remarked in tidal observations? The precipitation also in this region would surely tend to raise the level. But I leave the solution of these matters to those who are competent to decide.

"In lat. 7° N., long. 45° W., a strong current sets East three to four miles per hour. For fourteen days I had mostly fresh breezes from East to E.b.N. and E.b.S., with all possible sail set and steering W.b.S. I had Massey's log towing constantly, showing some days 110 miles in twenty-four hours. I at first supposed the watches were wrong. I could not believe that a current of such velocity could have existed in that quarter. At last I got an observation, which convinced me it was a current retarding our progress. I then steered to S.W., and in twenty-four hours was out of it, and found another setting W.N.W., which speedily took us in with the land. The breadth of this stream is about 120 miles, and runs strongest in lat. 6° N."

The Westerly Drift.—This surface current, apparently caused by the N.E. Trade wind, appears to extend from the Counter Equatorial current to 25° or 30° N., and from about 300 miles off the African coast to the West India Islands. Between 20° W. and 30° W. the set is to the S.W., and beyond 30° W. nearly due West. As it approaches the Gulf Stream, South of Bermuda, it is deflected to the southward, forming a counter-current on its eastern border, and trending to the S.E. outside the Bahama Islands.

Velocity: Between 30° and 20° N. the average appears to be from 8 to 20 miles a day. South of that from 11 to 36.

Current of the Caribbean Sea and Gulf of Mexico.—In the Caribbean Sea no constant currents have been observed; and although in the midst of this sea and about the islands which bound it on the East and North variable currents are found, but generally setting westward, yet along the coast the general current still prevails, following the direction of the coast at a variable distance. Thus it flows from East to West between the Island of Trinidad and Cape Agulhas; thence it proceeds W.N.W. and N.W. as far as Cape Catoche, crossing the Gulfs of Darien and Nicaragua and the Bay of Honduras; then it takes a complete circuit of the Gulf of Mexico. Thus, after reaching Cape Catoche it turns westward towards the shores of Campeche, along the coast of Yucatan; it thence continues towards Vera Cruz, changes its direction, and flows northward as far as the Rio del Norte, and even beyond that river; it flows afterwards N.E. till it meets the waters of the Mississippi; then takes a S.E. direction towards the Tortugas. At this point its direction becomes East, then N.E., and, lastly, North, following the Florida Channel, and discharging a second branch across the Bahama Islands that loses itself in the Atlantic Ocean.

In the middle of the Gulf of Mexico the waters do not appear to follow any particular course, as is the case in the Caribbean Sea, and they most frequently depend, as to strength and duration, on the prevailing winds.

On the coasts of Venezuela it has been observed that in the months of September, October, and

November, there is a counter-current which flows towards the East for a fortnight or three weeks at a time, the velocity of which is sometimes as much as 2 knots an hour. At the same period a similar counter-current running to the eastward is occasionally found on the South coasts of Cuba, Jamaica, San Domingo, and Porto Rico.

The temperature of the sea of this archipelago has been generally found higher than that of the ocean in the same latitude; but, notwithstanding the increase of caloric carried to its water by the surrounding continents, it is considered that the high temperature of the Caribbean Sea arises in a great measure from the currents of heated water that penetrate it from the torrid zone of the North Atlantic Ocean.

Gulf Stream or Florida Current.—The Gulf Stream has its origin in the Gulf of Mexico, and the waters having been heated there flow across to the Bahama Channel. Issuing from this strait they flow along the coast of Florida, and from 31° N. lat., take a N.E. direction as far as Cape Hatteras. There from the indentation of the coast the West limit of the current takes a more northerly direction, while its principal stream is still directed N.E. until it reaches the shoals of St. George and Nantucket, where its direction becomes more easterly. Soon after its direction is E.b.N., passing the southern extremity of the great bank of Newfoundland; and it preserves this direction, between 39° and 43° N. lat., till it reaches the meridian of 40° W. There a portion of it turns towards the South, and afterwards passing the archipelago of the Azores loses itself in the ocean. The warm waters of the stream, however, continue their drift to the eastward until they reach the coast of Europe.

The length of the Gulf Stream is about 3,000 miles from its source to its termination as a well-defined stream West of the Azores. It traverses in this course nearly twenty degrees of latitude,—from the parallel of 23° to that of 43°.

Velocity.—According to modern observation the velocity of this stream is much less than many authorities had previously estimated—and it is found to vary with the seasons—being strongest when the sun is North of the Equator.

In the narrows of the Florida Strait it reaches its highest velocity—sometimes 5 knots an hour—after leaving the strait it gradually reduces its speed from 90 miles a day to about 25 South of the bank of Newfoundland.

An exceptional rate of 4 knots an hour in August has, however, been reported off the S.E. extremity of that bank.

The western edge of the stream is found to be the strongest.

Its velocity afterwards diminishes rapidly, when it curves to the South; near the Azores it does not average more than 15 miles a day.

Temperature.---The mean temperature observed in the waters of the Gulf Stream in the Florida Strait is 85°, which makes it 6° above that of the ocean under the same parallel; ten degrees further North it is found to be 75°, having in this space diminished about 10°; in 61° W. long. it is found to be 78° in the summer, and 73° in winter; in 43° W. long. 75°; and in 38° W. long. 73°. Thus the temperature appears to decrease with the velocity, but not so quickly, as the waters advance eastward; but they still have a very high temperature when they turn towards the South. On coming out of the Bahama Channel, the waters of the Gulf Stream have a blue tinge, and the line of their separation from the waters of the Atlantic is perfectly evident for the space of a hundred miles.

N.E. Branch of the Gulf Stream.—At the place where the Gulf Stream curves towards the S.E. in 36° W. long., a portion of it, about 400 miles in width, continues as a considerable branch towards the N.E., passing between Iceland and the coast of Norway and surrounding the Feroe Isles. The water of this current is warm, and its temperature in summer has been estimated at 54°; in winter at 51°. Its direction is N.E.; but there are very few data as to its velocity. This current is important to ships bound from the Atlantic to Norway, Denmark, or to places situated on the northern coast of Europe.

Arctic Current.—It is considered that the Arctic current takes its rise in the frozen regions surrounding the North Pole: from whence one stream descends along the East coast of Greenland towards Cape Farewell. It passes round the cape, proceeding N.W. along the West coast of Greenland till it reaches the latitude of 63° N.; it then turns, and joining the stream coming down Davis' Strait, flows towards the South, along the coast of Labrador, forming the current known by the name of the Labrador current. It frequently attains a velocity of 36 miles a day, but the average appears to be about 15 miles.

On arriving at the North extremity of Newfoundland it sends a branch through the strait of Belle Isle, which mingles with the waters of the St. Lawrence and runs along the South coast of Newfoundland, while the principal current continues down the East coast and over the banks of Newfoundland.

It here meets the northern edge of the Gulf Stream, the great difference of temperature of the two currents causing those dense fogs which are so prevalent in this region.

The velocity across the banks varies greatly, and near the South coast of Newfoundland the current becomes very variable, and there is generally a strong indraught towards the land.

Flowing towards S.W., past the island of Nantucket, it then forms the counter-current of the United States coast, occupying the space comprised between the Gulf Stream and the coast extending to the entrance of the Florida Strait.

Immense masses of ice are brought from the Polar regions by this current, forming extensive fields and bergs, which are met with during the summer months within a radius of 400 miles from Cape Race.

This current facilitates very much the navigation of the coast of the United States from the northward. It is a cold current, as we have said, and consequently it will be easy to keep in it by means of thermometrical observations, and also to avoid entering the Gulf Stream.

Although to the West of the Azores the current of the Gulf Stream turns partly towards the South, yet between these islands and the coast of Europe a general movement of the waters from West to East continues. This current is known to mariners by the name of the "Bay current." Whether this current is a continuation of the Gulf Stream, or is occasioned by the intermixing of the Polar current with it, is a question which has not yet been solved.

The rapidity of the Bay current is very variable, ranging from 6 to 36 miles a day. In the latitude of Cape Finisterre the direction of it is E.S.E. to S.E., and it divides into two branches; one forming the Rennel current, the other that of the coast of Portugal.

The Rennel Current.—The Rennel current, which bears the name of the learned Major who first discovered its course, has an easterly direction near Cape Finisterre. It flows along the North coast of Spain, then proceeds North along the West coast of France, where it is felt at 30 or 40 miles off shore, and is 15 or 20 miles across. It has been found to run from one-half to two-thirds of a mile per hour. It is very variable, according to the strength of the wind and its direction. It is sometimes found to flow at the rate of a mile an hour and more, and to this current is attributed the loss of many vessels in the English Channel. It becomes wider as it proceeds northward; and in the latitude of Brest it is 80 miles across, and its direction nearly N.W. It issues from the Bay of Biscay, passes West of Ushant at 15 or 20 miles from that island, crosses the entrance of the Channel, and takes a westerly direction from the Scilly Isles. At the entrance of the Irish Sea it discharges a second branch into that sea, the principal branch flowing W.N.W. and West, towards Cape Clear, and losing itself off the coast of Ireland in the prevailing easterly drift.

The Portugal Current.—The southern branch of the Bay current, called the Portugal current, flows from Cape Finisterre towards the S.S.E. and S.E. along the coast. Off Cape St. Vincent its direction becomes S.E., and proceeding South, it becomes more and more easterly towards the Strait of Gibraltar, towards which all the waters comprised between Cape St. Vincent on the North, and Cape Cantin on the South, are directed, forming the Strait current, which carries the waters of the ocean into the Mediterranean.

The velocity of the Portugal current has been found to be from 12 to 24 miles a day. It is very variable, according to the prevailing winds, their strength and duration. This current, then, on the coast must never be trusted, especially in the winter or with strong N.W. winds, when it is necessary to keep well off the coast. The same attention also must be paid to the current generally of the Bay of Biscay, known as the Bay current, and that of Rennel.

These two currents are strong when the West winds, changing from N.W. to S.W., have continued long and with force. In this case it will be prudent to look out for the approaches of the English Channel, and on leaving the Bay of Biscay to double Cape Finisterre well out to seaward.

It is very important to note the fact that while at sea the waters are setting to the East, E.S.E., and S.E., as proved by a number of bottles found near Bayonne and the Basin of Arcachon, the waters of the interior and near the coast of France make their escape towards the North and N.W.

North African and Guinea Current.—The North African current would appear to be formed by the Polar current, which, after passing under the warm Gulf Stream, gradually comes to the surface and pursues its course towards the Equator, skirting the western coast of North Africa.

Between Cape St. Vincent and Cape Cantin, Morocco, the entire mass of water flows to the eastward towards the Strait of Gibraltar; through which the waters stream into the basin of the Mediterranean. From Cape Cantin to Cape Bojador, between Madeira and the archipelago of the Canaries, it is directed more southerly and S.E.; but it does not extend in this part and in this direction further out than 300 miles from the coast. Further out at sea its direction is South and S.S.W. From the archipelago of the Canaries to Cape Verd its direction is generally from South to S.S.W. Afterwards, from Cape Verd, it flows southward, a little easterly, following the coast of Africa, and takes the name of the Guinea current, and being joined by the Counter Equatorial current, it pursues its way with augmented force round Cape Palmas into the Bights.

The western limit of this current, according to some authorities, near Cape Verd, is between the island of Sal and that of San Nicolas; afterwards between the island of Mayo and that of Santiago, in the archipelago of the Cape Verd Islands. Its direction is from South to S.W. nearly all throughout its course from its rising till it reaches this part. Off Cape Mesurado its direction becomes E.S.E., and even East out at sea; while at a little distance from the coast it is S.E. as far as Cape Palmas. Off this cape its direction out at sea is easterly; then E.S.E. as far as the Gulfs of Benin and Biafra. It then meets with the Equatorial current, and after having reached Princes Island the waters of the two streams cease to be distinguishable as separate currents.

Captain J. B. Kennedy makes the following important observations in the *Nautical Magazine* on the current of the Cape Verd Islands:—

"While I lay at St. Vincent, a circumstance happened that I think cannot be too well known among navigators, as no doubt many of them are disposed to doubt the strength of the currents among these islands. The American ship *Borodino* arrived off the East end of St. Antonio early one night in June, and hauled her wind to wait for daylight. Shortly afterwards it fell calm, and the ship was drifted by the current over to St. Vincent, and had to let go an anchor in 40 fathoms water to prevent her being driven on to the rocks. At daylight next morning a breeze sprung up, and she slipped her chain and came to an anchor at Porto Grande. Her commander (Captain Flower) told me that while he was at anchor he hove the log and found the current setting three knots per hour. In this instance there can be no mistake about a current.

"A few days previously I had worked to windward from five p.m. until six a.m., with three topsails, jib, and mizen, and did not find any lee current. But the case of the *Borodino* shows that sometimes a most dangerous current is running amongst those islands."

But the currents among these islands are most uncertain in their force and direction, requiring the utmost vigilance on the part of the navigator.

Extent.—The breadth of the Guinea current varies according to the seasons. On the meridian of Cape Palmas it is nearly 150 miles across; but to the East, in the Gulf of Benin, it attains to a considerable breadth, nearly 300 miles from North to South. It is not felt in the vicinity of Isle St. Thomas, neither is the Equatorial current, which is only first found a little to the West of this island, in about 5° 30′ E. long.

Velocity.—The velocity of the current of North Africa, near its origin on the coast of Portugal, is about 12 miles a day. On the coast of Africa it varies from 10 to 24 miles, till it reaches Cape Verd.

Velocity of the Guinea Current.—This current flows with the greatest rapidity from June to September. Off Cape Palmas this is found to be 40 or 50 miles a day, and a few miles off shore it runs as much as 3 knots an hour. Near Cape Three Points it is about

40 miles per day. It then decreases, and in the Gulf of Benin its direction is from East southwardly.

Temperature.—Near the Cape Verd Islands, the temperature of the waters of this current is 8° or 10° below that of the adjacent ocean; it then increases rapidly in proportion as it proceeds South. In the Gulf of Guinea the temperature of the water has been observed to be 84° in the middle of the current; 83° and 81° at its southern limit in contact with the colder waters of the Equatorial current; it is 79° or 81° in the North part, adjoining the coast. This current is of the utmost importance in navigating the western coast of Africa.

Such are the general currents of the North Atlantic Ocean, the other portions of which are occupied by variable currents, the principal of which as above stated, is that flowing towards the West and S.W., caused by the constant Trade winds from N.E.

Brazil Current.—We have already spoken of the current of Brazil, a southern branch of the Equatorial current, dividing at Cape San Roque. It extends along the coast of South America from 6° or 7° S. to about 40° S.

The space between the coast and this current is occupied by other currents which follow the direction given to them by the alternate S.E. and N.E. winds of the coast of Brazil. The current of Brazil is crossed by the waters of the River Plata, which may be recognised more than 200 miles from the mouth of that river. Its waters do not, however, appear to produce much effect on the Brazil current, which, after passing Trinidad, seems to divide into two branches. The most considerable, taking an easterly direction, forms the counter-current of the South Atlantic Ocean. The other branch, flowing southward, forms a current which, though very feeble, is sometimes felt as far as the entrance of the Strait of Magellan. The mean velocity of this current in the part nearest the Equator, is about 20 miles a day.

Alternate Currents of the Coast of Brazil.—We have said that between the coast of Brazil and the current of which we have spoken alternate currents are met with, occasioned by the periodical winds which blow on this coast. The force of these currents depends on the strength of the wind, and consequently is very variable. From March to September, when winds from S.E. to E.S.E. prevail, the current sets northward, attaining in July its greatest velocity, about 48 miles a day, and from September to March, with N.E. winds, veering to E.N.E., it sets southward at a rate of about 25 to 36 miles a day; but these directions are much varied by the form of the coasts. Between Cape Frio and the La Plata with N.E. winds the current runs southward sometimes 40 miles a day; a S.E. wind drives it towards the shore. This current is felt only about 50 or 60 leagues from the coast of Brazil, and is of the utmost importance to navigation.

Current of Cape Horn.—The current off Cape Horn sets constantly from the Antarctic Sea and round the Cape from the Pacific Ocean into the Atlantic, and is generally accompanied by strong westerly gales.

Its general direction is E.N.E. and N.E. However constant may be the prevailing winds on the East coast of America, it flows to N.E., passing the Falkland Isles. In some seasons it preserves its N.E. direction as far as the parallel of 49° or 48° S. lat., and it is most probable that it joins the counter-current of the South Atlantic Ocean, of which we shall speak presently.

On the coasts of Terra del Fuego the rate of this current has been found to be 12 and 15 miles in the course of the day. In 57° S. lat. and 72° W. long. it is 42 miles. Near the coast its mean rate is about 24 miles, while between Cape Horn and Staten Land, in 55° S. lat., its direction is N.E., and its rate 56 miles per day.

The waters of this current, flowing northward and partly coming from the Antarctic Polar Sea, have a lower temperature than those of the adjacent ocean.

That part of the South Atlantic occupied by the counter-current which flows from the coast of Brazil towards the Cape of Good Hope, is only partially known. This current is considered in a great measure to be formed by the tropical current of the coast of Brazil, supplemented by the drift from the Cape Horn current. It flows to the eastward at the rate of from 12 to 30 miles a day, passing 150 or 180 miles South of the Cape of Good Hope. It then penetrates the Indian Ocean, and traces of it are found more than 2,000 miles beyond the Cape, where it unites with the Polar current of Australia. This current is very favourable to ships rounding the Cape to the eastward.

The Agulhas Current.—This current off the Cape of Good Hope is formed of two others from the Indian Ocean; the principal of which flows southward from the Mozambique Channel along the African coast; the other coming from that part of the ocean southward of Madagascar, is the S.W. branch of the Equatorial current of the Indian Ocean. These two Indian Ocean currents unite a little South of Port Natal, where they take a more southerly direction over and outside the bank of Agulhas, running at times 3 or 4 knots an hour. Instead of then flowing entirely, as one might imagine, into the Atlantic Ocean, it is arrested by the Polar water coming from the S.W., and the greater part of it is turned sharply back into the Indian Ocean, forming the Agulhas counter-current which runs at the rate of 36 to 60 miles a day.

The remainder of it turns to the N.W. and joins the South Atlantic Polar current setting towards the Equator.

Temperature.—On the meridian of Cape Agulhas the temperature of this current ranges from 68° in summer to 61° in winter. To the eastward the temperature remains higher.

Bands of this warm water alternating with the cold opposing current are found between 22° and 26° E., extending South from the edge of the bank to 44° S., and in this region heavy seas and tempestuous weather are caused by the violence of the conflicting currents.

South Atlantic Polar Current.—The counter-current of the South Atlantic joined to the drift from Cape

Horn and the Antarctic region, on meeting the Agulhas current off the Cape, divides into two branches, the southern continuing its course past the Cape into the South Indian Ocean; the other joining the N.W. branch of the Agulhas current, turns to the North and runs towards the Equator parallel to the West coast of Africa—the surface stream influenced by the S.E. Trade deviates to the westward, but from the indications of temperature, it seems certain that the main current continues its course northward as far as the Congo, North of which it commences to turn to the West and merges into the Equatorial current.

Velocity.—The rate of this current has been found off the Cape as much as 42 miles in twenty-four hours. North of this it varies from 12 to 30. In its course it receives the waters of the River Congo, flowing with great rapidity; but they do not appear to attain any decided influence over it, the direction of it and those of the current forming no considerable angle. The waters of the Amazon even do not mingle with the ocean for a considerable distance, and at 200 miles from the river's mouth the more highly coloured water of the Congo may be perceived.

Temperature.—Near the Cape of Good Hope the temperature of this current is as low as 51°, gradually increasing as it proceeds northward.

Off Cape Lopez a portion of the principal current takes a more northerly direction, following the coast of Gaboon as far as the Gulf of Biafra. The principal direction it takes is N.N.E. and N.E. near the coast, and N.W. further at sea and near the isles of the

Gulf of Biafra. At sea the limit of this current appears to be to the eastward of Princes Island.

Velocity.—The velocity of it is often 24 miles a day, but is generally about 10: it is, however, very variable, sometimes ceasing altogether. Still southerly currents are found in this part of the Gulf of Guinea, but the circumstance is very rare.

The knowledge of this northerly current is very useful to vessels sailing towards Gaboon.

The vast portion of sea forming the centre of the South Atlantic is occupied by currents produced by the S.E. Trade wind: their general direction varies from West to S.W. and S.S.W. in proportion as the waters approach the exterior limit of the current of Brazil, with which they mingle in order to return eastward by the cross current of the Atlantic.

CHAPTER IX.

General Remarks on the Navigation of the Atlantic.

Having treated on the prevailing winds and currents of the Atlantic Ocean, we shall now allude to the routes adopted in crossing it.

It is a general rule in the navigation of this ocean when going from East to West to attain, if convenient, the zone of the Trade winds; and to avoid it when going in the opposite direction. In the first case, then, it becomes desirable to reach it, and in the other to leave it, as soon as possible.

Routes from Europe to North America.—In the routes from Europe to North America, it is generally acknowledged that the farther North the port of departure is, the greater are the chances of a speedy passage.

In the beginning of the year it is advisable to keep North of 46° or 47° N. lat. as far as the meridian of about 36° W., and then to haul gradually to the southward until on the parallel of 43° N., and to keep in or near this parallel without making northing, especially in approaching the coast of North America, in order to pass well clear of Sable Island, this being so dangerous that it cannot be avoided too carefully. By following this route the northern limit of the Gulf Stream will be avoided, and after leaving Newfoundland the Arctic current will assist in the course to the S.W. for the ports of Nova Scotia and New Brunswick, or those of the North United States.

Towards the end of the year it may be better to adopt a course to the northward of that. Thus, leaving Europe, proceed to the N.W. as far as 55° latitude and 30° W. longitude. From thence cross the banks of Newfoundland on a S.W. course in 46° latitude; then pass about 60 miles South of Sable Island, and from thence make for the desired port.

In these passages it is recommended never to pass northward of Sable Island, on account of the frequent fogs met with in those regions, and the strong S.W. currents that are found near it, as well as the strong indraught between the extremes of the island on its northern side, the effects of which cannot be foreseen.

Vessels bound to the Gulf of St. Lawrence, unless intending to go through the Strait of Belle Isle, should, when South of the Virgin Rocks, make a course to pass to the southward of St. Pierre, and proceed about midway between Cape Breton and Newfoundland.

Routes from Europe to the Ports of the United States.—Passages from Europe to the United States are much retarded by the Gulf Stream, which should be avoided, for in case of contrary winds or calms an easterly set would be inevitable. In order to reach these ports, then, the routes previously indicated should be followed, passing southward of Sable Island, and from thence following in the southerly current which flows along the coast of the United States, in order to avoid that of the Gulf Stream. In all cases if this current is to be crossed to the westward it should be done as quickly as possible.

On this northern route the greatest vigilance should be used, in order to avoid ice after passing 30° W.

There is another route which, although longer as to distance, appears preferable; for if the time occupied in the passage might appear greater, in consequence of the distance, it is really less as to the speed with which the vessel would sail from port to port. This route is that of the Trade winds. On leaving Europe, if the wind be not favourable to a direct route towards the ports of the United States, it would be better to make good a course South or S.W., as the wind permits, in order to find the Trade winds as quickly as possible. The best course to reach their latitude is either between the Azores and Madeira, or Madeira and the Canaries. It would be better to avoid passing between these last named islands and the coast of Africa, because the Trade wind there loses its force and direction. But a vessel when once in the region of the Trade winds may pursue the most convenient course, according to her desired port, only being cautious as to making the land, and in crossing the Gulf Stream, so as to be about 10 leagues or so to windward of her port.

There are, however, many circumstances under which this route can be made without the assistance of the Trade winds, and they occur principally during the 40 or 50 days after the two equinoxes, periods in which N.E. winds are frequently found; so that vessels sailing then may shape their course at once. Besides, if a vessel in the counter-current of the Atlantic meet with contrary winds, it is better to make southing, in order to fall in with the Trade, than to be striving against these winds. In the spring, summer, and autumn seasons, when the N.E. Trade winds extend as far as 28° and 30° N. lat., the passage by these winds will be advantageous. Lastly, if the wind admits of it when going from Europe to the United States, West is the course to adopt; if not, and if at the time of the equinoxes, choose that which is nearest to it. In any other case we should prefer adopting a southern course, so as to atttain the region of the Trade winds. These remarks also apply to vessels bound to Bermuda.

Homeward Course from the United States to Europe. —In the homeward course from the ports of the United States to Europe, those currents which set to the southward should be crossed as quickly as possible, so as to gain the Gulf Stream and attain a northern latitude in order to get clear of this current, because it is frequently subject to bad weather; and in the months of July, August, September, and October, severe weather is experienced in it. During the other months, however, probably a good vessel might keep in it, and would thereby much shorten her passage. When on the meridian of 42° W., the course should be directed so as to pass to the northward of the

Azores; and from thence, according to the winds, to follow the course most convenient for reaching the port of destination. These passages are greatly assisted by West winds, veering to S.W. and N.W.

The passages by sailing ships between the northern ports of Europe and New York, &c., vary slightly, according to the time of year, but the following are the average number of days occupied :—

Europe to America :—

January to March............	35 days.
April to June................	34 ,,
July to September............	33 ,,
October to December	35 ,,

America to Europe :—

January to March............	22 days.
April to June................	23 ,,
July to September............	23 ,,
October to December	22 ,,

In leaving Europe for the Gulf of Mexico or for ports of the Caribbean Sea, as soon as an offing is obtained, the course should be S.W., in order to reach the region of the N.E. Trade winds as soon as possible. In this part of the route, when nearing the African coast, due allowance must be made for the easterly set caused by the prevailing westerly winds and the North African current. If obliged to continue as far South as the Canaries to find the Trade they should be left to the eastward.

Captain Kennedy, to whose important information we have already alluded, speaks thus of the passage to New York from the Equator in the *Nautical Magazine.* He says :—

"Last winter I was bound from India to New York, and I read with attention Maury's remarks upon the Gulf Stream. I steered N.W. across the stream to make the land about Cape Lookout, but in the middle of the stream was caught in a heavy S.E. gale. I then hauled up for Cape Hatteras under close-reefed topsails and fore sail, taking the temperature of the water every ten minutes. At ten minutes past midnight the temperature of the water fell 4°, and five minutes afterwards 2° more, namely, from 76° to 70°, and in another ten minutes down to 68°. The wind had hauled round to the southward, and I kept the ship up E.b.N., and in twenty minutes had the water thermometer up to 76° again. To test the truth of Maury's 'wall of cold water,' I twice kept the ship off North, and in ten or fifteen minutes the temperature of the water fell to 67°, and I then hauled up East, and in about the same time we again had it up to 76°. I was aware that the stream was forced inshore by a S.E. gale, so, being afraid of the shoals off Hatteras, I hove to at 2h. a.m.

"I was twenty days, in December and January last, beating about between Cape Hatteras and New York, and as we are likely to have some ships cruising on that station, I will offer a few remarks. Blunt's *Coast Pilot* is the best book of directions; Maury's coloured chart of the approaches towards New York is very valuable. I found the water thermometer an infallible guide as to when we got on soundings; invariably the temperature of the water fell 5° when we came into 50 fathoms, and when the ship was inside of

20 fathoms the temperature of the water was 2° lower sometimes, but generally the same as the air. Steering N.W. from the Gulf Stream with the temperature of the water 76°, we came to 67°, shortly after to 60°, and when in 50 fathoms, on the parallel of Cape Charles, the water thermometer showed 45°; this difference was run in a few hours. In a short time we were so certain of the ship's position by the changes in the temperature of the water, that my officers have frequently reported to me that the ship was on soundings, and on inquiry I have found that they had not had a cast of the lead, but judged by the water thermometer.

"The soundings between Cape Hatteras and Long Island are so regular and so well laid down in Maury's chart that no man could be in doubt of his position if he only made use of his lead. Either in making a passage to New York from the southward or in cruising on the coast in winter, a ship should get inside the Gulf Stream as soon as she rounds Hatteras. A current nearly always sets towards the mouth of the Chesapeake, between the latitudes of Cape Henry and Barnegat. When it sets in for a regular winter gale from the N.W., a ship has smooth water by keeping inshore between 20 fathoms and 40 miles outside that. If she is further off than that the sea is very heavy. Winds from the eastward nearly always bring wet and thick weather. The deep sea lead is almost the only pilot required on the above-named coast.

"The Americans thoroughly understand the way to navigate their own coast, and no ship of any kind ever neglects the use of the water thermometer. It is to them what the lead is to us in the Channel."

A vessel once in the region of the Trade winds, bound to the lesser Antilles, may make directly for her port, keeping as long as possible on the parallel of 19° or 20° North latitude, from the month of May to December. From December to June, on the contrary, a more southern track should be followed. But in approaching the Antilles much allowance must be made for the current, as the dead reckoning will always place the vessel *East* of her true position. In such cases it will be well to add twelve miles a day to her supposed western progress to allow for this current. If the vessel be destined for the Great Antilles or the ports of the Gulf of Mexico she will enter the Caribbean Sea between Guadaloupe and Antigua, or between Isle St. Martin and Culebra. This is invariably the entrance chosen in voyages to St. Thomas, Porto Rico, Kingston, Havana, Tampico, Vera Cruz, and New Orleans. When bound to La Guayra, Porto Bello, Cartagena, or any of the ports of Venezuela, vessels generally pass between St. Lucia and St. Vincent. Vessels bound for Guiana should keep inshore and to the South of their destined port on account of the currents.

Routes from Europe to South America.—On leaving Europe for Guiana, the general route, from November to July, will be to cross the parallel of 10° N. lat., in the most direct line between the meridians of 48° and 50° W., in order to cross the zone of calms to the West of the most difficult part. Having reached the parallel of 10° they would keep a point or a point and a half further South to meet the effect of the general current setting N.W., so as to attain, at about 50 leagues from land, the parallel of 3° or 3° 30′ N. latitude. A westerly course, until in about eight or ten fathoms, might be adopted for the coast. From July to November the following course might be better adopted and sometimes with advantage. Passing 150 leagues to the West of the Cape Verd Islands, steer South, so as to cross the zone of the variables, and reach the S.E. Trade, which at this season is felt as far as 5° and 6° or even 7° or 8° N. latitude. Having found the S.E. Trade, a westerly course between the Equator and 3° 30′ N. latitude would make the coast in a depth of six or eight fathoms.

Vessels from the Lesser Antilles bound to Europe generally pass between Guadaloupe and Montserrat. From thence, with East and N.E. winds, it is best to make northing, in order to get clear of the Trade winds as soon as possible. When the zone of the variable winds is attained, a ship should proceed as previously directed in the homeward routes from North America to Europe. Vessels from Jamaica generally pass between St. Domingo and Cuba, and thence between Inagua and Crooked Island, but in many cases it is preferable to run round the western end of Cuba and take advantage of the Gulf Stream to gain the Atlantic. If bound to the Lesser Antilles a vessel should steer between the North coast of St. Domingo and the S.E. shore of the Bahamas. From thence, avoiding the wind, she could reach the Lesser Antilles sooner than by plying to windward in the Caribbean Sea. Vessels from La Guayra, Porto Bello, or Cumana for Europe leave the Caribbean Sea by the Mona Passage, formed by the Isles of St. Domingo and Porto Rico. From thence they proceed to the N.E., in order to cross the parallel of 40° N. latitude between the meridian of 30° and 35° W. longitude.

Ships leaving Porto Rico proceed directly North, in order to pass the region of the Trade winds, following nearly the same route. On leaving Cuba or the ports in the Gulf of Mexico, vessels pass up the Bahama Channel and thence steer to N.E. to leave the stream. They then proceed eastward, passing South of the Bermudas, and again cross the Gulf Stream in the neighbourhood of the Azores.

Vessels leaving the ports of Costa Firma for the Lesser Antilles, will perhaps derive advantage from adopting the Bahama Channel instead of contending against the wind in the Caribbean Sea.

Outward Voyage.—Elbe to Havana, 59 days; Hamburg to Guayra, 50 days; Channel to St. Domingo, 46 days; Channel to Vera Cruz, 40 days; Channel to Antigua, 27 days.

Homeward Voyage.—Havana to Elbe, 49 days; Jamaica to Channel, 32 days; Havana to Gibraltar, 47 days; Vera Cruz to London, 42 days; Guadaloupe to Channel, 33 days; Port au Prince to Channel, 30 days; St. Thomas to Hamburg, 45 days.

Routes from Europe to Rio.—Steam vessels make this passage as direct as possible, but sailing vessels leaving the Channel for ports of South America, such as Rio Janeiro or Buenos Ayres, when well clear of the Bay of Biscay, ought to steer about South-West to fall in with the N.E. Trade wind as soon as possible, passing between the Azores and Madeira, or between Madeira and the Canaries, and to the West of this archipelago, unless required to stop here. Thence they would proceed to cross the line, traversing the zone of the variable winds.

Crossing the Line.—It has been for some time the rule to cross the line in 22° or 25° W. longitude. Numerous records have proved it preferable to cross it between 25° and 30° W., from October to April, and between 20° and 26° from May to September. In fact, between these meridians the zone of the variable winds of the Equator is less extended than it is towards the coast of Africa, and it is frequently passed without experiencing calms, the N.E. and S.E. Trade winds almost joining each other.

The best longitude for outward bound ships to cross the Equator has, however, always been a disputed question among navigators. The following is an abstract of passages across the line, compiled by the Meteorological Office from the records of 930 ships :—

	E. of 20°	20° to 24°	24° to 28°	W. of 28°.
Jan., Feb., March	15	46	99	48
April, May, June	8	61	93	55
July, Aug., Sept.	35	64	106	66
Oct., Nov., Dec.	4	23	91	116
Total............	62	194	389	285

Captain Toynbee recommends the following as the best monthly routes for outward bound ships to cross the line:—

Jan. ..	26° to 27°	....	Feb. ..	27° to 28°	....	March ..	27° to 28°
April ..	27° to 28°	....	May ..	24° to 25°	....	June	25° to 27°
July....	25° to 28°	....	Aug. ..	24° to 26°	....	Sept.	24° to 26°
Oct.	26° to 28°	....	Nov. ..	28° to 29°	....	Dec.	28° to 29°

and for vessels bound North to cross as follows:—

March, 26° to 30°; July, 20° to 30°; and during the rest of the year between 25° and 30°.

Great care should be taken when in the vicinity of St. Paul's rocks, as they can only be seen a short distance off, and a very strong westerly current runs past.

As to the fear of being drawn towards the West and towards Cape St. Roque by the Equatorial current, it would seem that this has been much exaggerated, and also that the Trade winds in this part blow more from the East than they were supposed to do, so that Cape St. Roque may be doubled without any difficulty. Still, dull sailing ships should avoid crossing the line too far to the westward. As a general rule it may be stated that the winds from the sea on the coast of Brazil blow nearly always at right angles to the line of the coast, principally from October to March. During this period, then, the coast South of Cape St. Roque may be approached without fear, the winds being generally from N.E. to E.N.E., and the current near the coast setting from North to South, thereby, as observed, assisting the passage. From March to October, on the contrary, the winds coming from East to E.S.E. and the current near the coast setting from the southward, it will be preferable to keep 40 or 50 leagues from the coast, in the Brazil current, and pass westward of Trinidad in order to reach Rio Janeiro and Buenos Ayres.

Vessels bound to the Pacific by Cape Horn, whether sailing from Rio Janeiro or Buenos Ayres, or coming from the northward, should keep within a distance of 100 miles from the coast of Patagonia, in order to avoid the high sea, caused by the West winds which prevail there, and to profit by the changes of the wind on the coast. They will then pass between the Falkland Islands and Terra del Fuego, and will generally pass East of Staten Land, the Strait of Le Maire being often difficult to adopt. The courses to be taken in leaving the ports of South America differ according to the latitude of these ports.

Homeward Voyage from South America to Europe.—Vessels from the ports of Brazil to the northward of the point of Olinda may generally stand along the coast on the starboard tack and direct to the northward. Those leaving any port of Brazil to the southward of that point are generally obliged to get on the port tack, to avoid the coast and make a board to the southward. Sometimes the N.E. winds oblige them to continue on this tack for 12 or 14 days, and standing to the S.E. and S.S.E. as far as 28° or even to 32° S. latitude. This tack should be kept as far as 32° W., so that on standing to the northward on the starboard tack a vessel may be certain of reaching to windward of the Isle of Trinidad. As the vessel proceeds northward the wind will be found more easterly, admitting a slack bowline, or it would be extraordinary if she does not weather Fernando de Noronha, crossing the line between the meridians of 25° and 30° W. From thence the zone of the variables of the Equator, generally West of the meridian of 32°, will be crossed, and the starboard tack is kept through the N.E. Trade as far as 30° N. latitude. Once beyond the region of the Trade winds the course must be shaped according to the destination, passing northward of the Azores.

After these observations concerning the ports of Brazil, there will be very little difficulty as to the course to be pursued in leaving the southern ports or coming from Cape Horn. The West winds which prevail in this zone will facilitate a vessel's progress to the limits of the S.E. Trade.

Outward Voyage.—The Channel to Rio Janeiro, 50 days; Channel to St. Catherine, 62 days; Straits of Gibraltar to St. Catherine, 53 days; Havre to Maranhao, 43 days; Marseilles to Rio Janeiro, 65 days; Bordeaux to Cape St. Augustine, 45 days; Bordeaux to Cape St. Antonio, 64 days; Rio Janeiro to St. Catherine, 6 days; Channel to Montevideo, 57 days; Channel to Cayenne, 31 days; Europe to Cape Horn, 82 days.

Homeward Voyage.—Montevideo to Rio Janeiro, 11 days; Rio Janeiro to the Channel, 58 days; Ports in the North of Brazil to Europe, 33 to 37 days; Montevideo to the Channel, 83 days; Maranhao to the Channel, 65 days; Cayenne to the Channel, 56 days; Cape Horn to Rio Janeiro, 18 days; Cape Horn to Europe, 73 days.

CHAPTER X.

Europe to Africa North of the Equator—The Canaries —Cape Verds—Routes to and from African Coast —St. Helena and Ascension.

The foregoing will suffice to give a general idea of the voyages from Europe to the coasts of South America. Let us now proceed with those from Europe to that part of the coast of Africa situated North of the Equator.

The commanders of vessels from the English Channel must bear in mind what has been said in regard to the currents of those parts. After having doubled Cape Finisterre, according to the time of year, at a distance of 35 or 60 leagues, a vessel should steer between South and S.W., giving the coast of Portugal a wide berth, especially during winter, in order to pass East or West of Madeira, or to reach the Canaries, which are always sighted by vessels on their passage to the coast of Africa. These islands may be passed on either side, the channel between them and the African coast presenting no danger which is not apparent. If it is desirable to pass through them, the preferable channel is that between Palma and Hiero on the West and by Gomera on the East.

It is rarely after having passed to the southward by the other channels that calms are not met with, along with a swell which endangers the masts under the lee of the large islands of the archipelago. This is especially the case with the wind from the North and N.E., which, interrupted by them, does not reunite in a steady course till far to the southward. In November and December it is preferable in bad weather to pass clear away to the westward of these islands in case of meeting the S.E. winds, which are frequent at that time.

If desirous of touching at the Canaries, the best anchorage for a ship is that of Palmas, North of the Grand Canary. The town there offers more resources than Santa Cruz, in Teneriffe, and the bay is easy to leave under sail in all weathers; which is not the case at Santa Cruz, a harbour generally frequented, though very dangerous with a S.E. wind.

On leaving the Canaries, a vessel bound to the coast southward of them will adopt a South, S.W., or S.S.W. course, according as she may have passed outside or through one of the channels of the group. Having passed the parallel of 19° at the southern extremity of the bank of Arguin, she would gradually haul to the eastward, thus getting into the North African current, in which she would keep her course. St. Louis should be made a little to the northward of its latitude. If bound for Goree, a vessel should pass round Cape Verd. When bound to places South of Goree, such as the Gambia or Sierra Leone, or even to the coast of Liberia, the route as far as Cape Verd will be the same; for a vessel must generally pass it unless leaving the Cape Verd Islands. In all these cases should a vessel not touch at the islands it is best to steer in such a manner as to pass nearer to Cape Verd than to the islands of that name, because the wind is steadier and fresher near the coast. From Cape Verd the navigation depends on circumstances, being comparatively easy with N.E. winds in the fine season, but difficult with the S.W. winds of winter.

Vessels proceeding to places on the coast of Guinea or to the isles of the Gulf of Biafra or the Gaboon, after having left Cape Verd will make for Cape Palmas, either with the favourable winds from October to May, or with the contrary ones principally during June, July, August, and September, when they blow from S.W., W.S.W., West, and W.N.W., interrupted by calms. At this period it is best to keep 100 leagues from the coast. They will then steer so as to sight the Cape or about 20 leagues or more to seaward of it. At this distance they will find the Guinea current, setting to the East and E.N.E. from 15° or 16° W. longitude. After reaching the parallel of Cape Palmas, they will find, as already stated, the wind from S.W. and W.S.W. Winds with a current will then be found favourable for reaching any of the places of North Guinea. But it must be observed that in these routes a vessel should not pass further South than 2° N. lat., in order not to get into the Equatorial current which sets to the westward. Thus, as soon as the parallel of Cape Palmas is reached and the cape sighted by a vessel bound to the

Gold Coast or the Ivory or Slave Coast, she should keep in the zone comprised between the coast of Guinea and 2° N. latitude.

The best method for a vessel to navigate this coast is to keep the land in sight, at about the distance of 10 or 15 miles, and to approach it to about the distance of one or two miles when 30 or 40 miles West of her destination, taking great care not to run beyond it. In estimating the route it will be very important to consider the velocity of the current—which runs from 20 to 40 miles a day—for it is requisite to approach it well to westward of the point to which she may be bound.

If bound for the islands of the Gulfs of Biafra or Benin, a vessel having doubled Cape Palmas should steer East, keeping between 3° and 2° N. lat. as long as possible, according to the island she is bound for. She should then cross obliquely the zone comprised between 2° N. lat. and the Equator, running before the wind for her port, in order to make the land to the southward of it. The same must be done in going to the islands of the Gulf of Biafra. In the vicinity of these islands the Coast current is met with, setting to the N.E., and sometimes N.N.E.; then S.S.W. winds will be found, veering, perhaps, to South as the Equator is approached. In sailing from Princes Island to Gaboon this current is crossed, setting N.E., N.W., and sometimes North. It is therefore necessary, in going from Princes Island to Gaboon, generally to make the land to the South of this river in order to counteract the effect of the current.

In the bottom of the Gulf of Biafra the currents are variable, though in the latitude of Fernando Po, and between this island and the coast, they generally set to E.N.E. and N.E. If from thence it is desired to proceed to the southward a vessel should keep at a little distance from the coast of Gaboon, in order to profit by the alternate breezes and to take advantage of the tides.

The Guinea current formerly terrified seamen, for they supposed that having once entered the gulf they could not leave it without much difficulty. These fears, as will be seen, were groundless.

Leaving a place eastward of Cape Palmas, a vessel should stand well out on the starboard tack till she is clear of the Guinea current and has entered the Equatorial; and, according to the time of year, she may cross the line to the southward for southerly winds. She may then get on the port tack, so as to reach well to the West of her port of destination, in order to allow for the effect of the Guinea current, which will be found in 2° N. latitude; and if she cannot make it so on this tack, she must go about in 2° N. lat., and stand out on the starboard tack again till she has gone far enough West to be sure of reaching the coast to the westward of her port. In a few days, by this method, the port will be gained. Vessels which have endeavoured to get to windward on the coast of Guinea, are sometimes 30 or 40 days in reaching Grand Bassam from Cape Coast, and have been obliged to give up the attempt and stand out to sea.

On leaving Fernando Po, a vessel must make her way along the coast of Gaboon, profiting by the slants of wind and current, and consequently keeping near the coast until she has made southing enough to stand into the Equatorial current. Leaving Princes Island she should take the starboard tack, with S.W. winds, and continue on that tack as far as the coast permits; she may then go on the port tack and thus get clear of the Gulf of Guinea.

If intending to leave the Gulf of Guinea, after reaching the Equator she may keep to the southward, profiting as she may by winds from South and S.S.W. to S.S.E., till she reach the meridian of Cape Palmas and in the case of intending to go to the northward, after reaching about 17° West, she may make for the Atlantic on a course according to her destination. Then, if returning to Europe, it will be best to leave the Equator in about 23° W. and make to the northward, and afterwards pursue the same route as that indicated in returning from Brazil to Europe; but if near the Equator, West and N.W. winds are found, which is often the case from May to September, the ship may then cross it in 17° or 18° W., and pass between the Cape Verd Isles and the coast of Africa. North of the Cape Verd Isles the N.E. Trade will be found, which will enable her to proceed on the starboard tack. If returning to any point on the coast of Africa, Sierra Leone, Gambia, Goree, or St. Louis, a northerly course must be taken in 16° or 17° W., and a course made good between the meridians of 22° and 28° W., in order to avoid entering into the polar current of North Africa until the parallel of the Bissagos is reached. This last course will be especially favourable from May to September, which is the winter season. Lastly, a vessel bound to the United States or the Antilles, should proceed North in 28° or 33° W. long.

Favourable Season for leaving the Gulf of Guinea.—The most favourable season for leaving the Gulf of Guinea is from May to December. A vessel is then seldom obliged to cross the line; the S.E. winds are generally well established at this period, and reach beyond the Equator. But from December to May it is better to cross the Equator, and proceed at least in 0° 30′ or 1° S. lat. By following the foregoing directions, a vessel will in a few days be clear of the Gulf of Guinea. In order to enter it, a vessel should pass near Cape Palmas, and keep in the North Guinea current, between the coast and 2° or 3° N. lat.

But in order to leave the Gulf of Guinea, as a general rule, a vessel should endeavour to reach the Equator by the most direct route according to her longitude. From May to December she may keep on the Equator, or a little North of it. During the other months it will be better to keep South of 30′ or 1° S. lat., and to the westward as far as the meridian of 16°, 17°, or 23° W. long., according to the port of destination in the North Atlantic Ocean.

Passages.—North of Europe to Madeira, 15 days; Strait of Gibraltar to Madeira, 4 to 5 days; North of Europe to the Canaries, 16 days; Strait of Gibraltar to Canaries, 7 days; North of Europe to Cape Verd

Islands, 28 days; North of Europe to Senegal, 18 days; North of Europe to Goree, 20 days; North of Europe to Gambia, 24 days.

On the coast of Africa, South of Senegal, the length of the voyage, according to the season, will vary greatly. Thus, in the fine season 29 days are taken to go from Goree to Princes Island, and in the winter generally 36 to 38 days.

Returning.—Princes Island to Goree, 38 to 40 days; Gambia to Goree, 3 to 4 days; Goree to Senegal, 5 to 7 days; Senegal to Channel, 30 to 40 days.

There are some instances of this voyage having been made in 24 and 22 days.

Routes from Europe to Ports of Africa South of the Equator.—The routes from Europe to those ports of Africa situated South of the Equator, are very different, according to the latitude of these ports. They are distinguished as the *Great Route* and the *Little Route.*

The Great Route is that adopted to reach the Cape of Good Hope, and in general all the ports situated South of Cape Negro.

The Little Route is that which ships take to reach ports situated North of Cape Negro.

The Great Route is, however, followed by many vessels bound to these ports. Vessels taking the Great Route, on leaving Europe will follow the directions given for the routes from Europe to Brazil; they will consequently cross the line between 23° and 28° W. Thence, profiting by the S.E. Trade, they will shape their course for the Isle of Trinidad. They will pass West of it, and making for the southward will find westerly winds and the counter current of the South Atlantic. They will then make for the Cape of Good Hope, so as to cross the parallel of 30° S. lat. near 18° W. long. By following these routes vessels have been only 59 days in sailing from the English Channel to Cape Town. A similar route may be adopted when bound to places on the West coast of Africa North of Cape Negro. Thus, after crossing the line between 23° and 28° W. long., a vessel may take the port tack with the S.E. Trade and stand on, so that when taking the other tack she may reach the coast to the southward of where she is bound to, and so counteract the effect of the African polar current setting to the northward along the West coast of this continent. But if destined for Benguela, Angola, or even a point North of Cape Negro, the course may be so modified as to render the passage shorter.

On leaving Europe a vessel intending to take the Little Route should shape her course so as to reach the Trade winds as soon as possible, passing either West or East of Madeira and West of the Canaries, or in the channels through those islands. Thence she should pass West of the Cape Verd Islands if in winter, that is to say from June to September. During the other months she would pass between those islands and Cape Verd, keeping closer to the cape than to the islands, because near the continent the winds from N.E. and N.N.W. are fresher and better established in this season. Whichever passage is adopted, after having passed South of Cape

Verd she would keep along the African coast, at the distance of 60 or 80 leagues, until the parallel of the Bissagos is passed. From thence she would steer for Cape Palmas, passing it at the distance of 20 leagues, and cross the Gulf of Guinea on the starboard tack. This tack will generally enable her to reach Cape Lopez, and often South of Anno Bon. She would then get on the other tack to look for the S.E. winds of the southern hemisphere, and keeping in the space comprised between the coast and the line passing from the Cape of Good Hope to Cape Palmas, she would again get her starboard tacks on board to fall in with the S.W. winds which prevail there and blow alternately from sea and land from January to September. She would then keep near land to profit by them. The sea breeze lasts during day from ten or eleven o'clock in the morning, blowing from W.S.W. to S.W.: the land breeze lasts the night, from S.E. to South. She would therefore manage her boards in such a manner as to be near the coast for the land wind at night, and to be at a distance from it in the morning for the sea breeze. This navigation is similar to that on the coast of Senegambia in the northern hemisphere; but here the coast is much more extended and the season from January to September is particularly favourable for it. In the rainy season near Cape Lopez squalls from the westward are sometimes met, but of short duration.

Routes from Europe to the Islands of the South Atlantic Ocean.—Vessels from Europe to the islands of the South Atlantic Ocean have been sometimes a hundred days on their passage. The following remarks on the subject may prove useful:—

To reach Ascension from the Channel a vessel should gain the N.E. Trade as soon as possible, and pass between the Cape Verd Islands and the continent, or else West of the Cape Verd Islands. From thence she would steer so as to double Cape Palmas and make it if she can. As soon as she has lost the N.E. Trade she should steer South to cross the zone of the variable winds without passing West of the meridian of 15° or 17° W. In approaching the limit of the S.E. Trade winds near Cape Palmas, and even North of this cape, winds from the S.W. will always be found and sometimes from W.S.W. With these she should get on the starboard tack and cross the line in 5° or 6° W. long., or even more to the eastward if she would improve her speed with the currents of the Gulf of Guinea. In this case she should make nearly the same course as shown for the islands of the Gulf of Biafra, keeping on the parallel of 2° N. in order to reach the Gulf of Guinea easily: then cross to the South, reaching Cape Lopez on the starboard tack. As soon as the South and S.E. winds are found she would get on the port tack and soon reach Ascension.

Routes to St. Helena.—There are two different routes from Europe to St. Helena. Considering the position of this island in the S.E. Trade it cannot be reached from North without first standing away to the East or West in order to run down on it. The quickness of the passage will depend generally on the time occupied in crossing the zone of the variable winds of the Equator. The season will therefore determine which of the routes it will be best to pursue. The western route may always be taken. That of the East is only advisable during the months of November, December, January, February, and March—a period when, as above said, the zone of the variable winds of the Equator is diminished. The eastern route during the months just mentioned will be the same as that followed in going to Ascension, only the course should be prolonged towards the coast of Africa until the wind fails. The other tack is then adopted and St. Helena is generally reached by this route more quickly than by the westerly one. But when the sun has North declination the eastern route becomes very uncertain and the western is preferable. It may, however, be taken for granted that a smart sailing ship holding a good wind may adopt the eastern route in all seasons. After having crossed the line between 23° and 28° W. long. a ship adopting the western route will have to get on the port tack. This will take her towards the coast of Brazil, and she must generally tack nearer to it than to St. Helena. On the starboard tack she will then make to the S.E. as far as 23° S. lat., she will then stand across the S.E. trade, and passing to windward of the island run round the East end to the anchorage.

The currents near St. Helena are not strong, and when the wind is favourable there will be little trouble in reaching the bay, except during the syzigies, when the N.W. current prevails.

The average voyage from Europe to the Cape of

Good Hope is about 80 days, to St. Helena, 60 days.

Routes from Ascension and St. Helena to the Coast of South Africa.—St. Philip de Benguela being one of the southernmost places reached from Ascension on the coast of Africa South of the Equator, we may adopt it, as from it all points to the northward will be easily attained. On leaving Ascension the starboard tack should be adopted, and in order not to fall into the great westerly current a vessel should endeavour not to pass North of the parallel of 4° S. lat., and also not to stand further South when the wind will not permit her to lay about S.E.b.S. true. This, however, will depend on circumstances. It will be easy to make a short board so as not to pass the above limits; but it will often happen that the passage may be made without tacking at all, because the winds in general along and near the African coast veer to S.W. and sometimes to W.S.W. A vessel from St. Helena one can understand has only to lay her head for the point of the coast she is bound for, or something to the South of it to allow for the polar current of the South Atlantic. And generally, notwithstanding the opinion of several authors who advise that on leaving these islands a vessel should take the port tack to get to the South and West when bound to a place on the coast of Africa as far North as St. Philip, we should take the starboard tack on leaving those islands, and steer for our destination, allowing for the effect of the current, which flows with a rapidity of 15 miles in 24 hours, to the N.W. and W.N.W.

But leaving Ascension or St. Helena for a more southern part, the Cape of Good Hope for instance, a vessel should adopt the port tack to make southing and stand towards the American coast, profiting then by the remarks made concerning the routes from Europe to the Cape of Good Hope in the southern hemisphere.

Routes from the Coast of Africa to Ascension and St. Helena.—The routes from ports on the coast of Africa to Ascension and St. Helena have been shown in coming from places North of the Equator; they are nearly the same as those followed in reaching them from Europe, whether the Great or Little Route is adopted. When a vessel leaves the coast of Africa from anywhere South of these Islands the winds and currents are favourable, and she should endeavour to make to windward of it, that is, more to the southward than to leeward.

Homeward Routes from the North Coast of Africa to Europe.—In referring to the navigation of the Gulf of Guinea the routes from thence to Europe have been alluded to. On reaching 23° W. long., standing to the South of the Equator, a vessel should then commence her northing on the starboard tack and cross the zone of the N.E. Trade winds. As soon as she has reached the zone of the variable winds she would make progress, passing to the North of the Azores or between them. A vessel starting from a point to the northward of Cape Palmas should get to the westward with S.W. winds which prevail in the vicinity of that cape, passing as quickly as possible through the zone of the variable winds of the Equator; she would then take the starboard tack with the N.E. Trades and make her northing. A vessel leaving the ports of Senegambia, the Gambia, Goree, or St. Louis, with N.E. and N.N.E. winds, during the fine season, would stand out on the starboard tack till she reached the zone of the variable winds. In the homeward routes from points on the West coast of Africa, South of the Equator, that from the Cape of Good Hope to Europe may serve for the rest.

Route from the Cape of Good Hope to Europe.—On coming from the Indian Ocean round the Cape of Good Hope, if in the fine season, a vessel may approach the land without fear and steer North when the Cape is passed. But if in the winter season, namely from June to September, before steering North it will be best to get an offing to the West of 40 or 50 leagues from the land, in case of meeting with West and N.W. winds, which prevail during this season. After doubling the Cape, in the fine season, namely from October to April, a vessel will pass near St. Helena, a short distance either to the East or West of it. From St. Helena she would steer N.W., in order to pass 12 or 13 miles East or West of Ascension, and thence cross the line between 23° and 28° W. long. The route she would then take has been previously pointed out in returning to Europe. In the case of doubling the Cape of Good Hope between August and September, a vessel should keep at a respectful distance from the coast and steer South of the zone of the S.E. Trade winds, in order to cross the parallel of 20° S. lat. on the meridian of about 18° W. long. She would then endeavour to cross the line between 26° and 28° W. long. In this season the average of many passages from the Cape of Good Hope to Europe is 70 days: from the Cape to St. Helena generally 15 days; and from St. Helena to Ascension generally 6 days.

Routes from the Ports of North America to the Coasts of North Africa.—From the ports of North America to that part of the coast of Africa North of the Equator, the course at first is nearly the same as that for returning to Europe; but when a vessel has reached far enough to the eastward to make her port, she would then steer for that part of the coast, crossing obliquely the region of the N.E. Trade winds.

Routes from North America to West Africa or South America.—When steering for any port of Africa South of the Equator, she would cross the zone of the N.E. Trades obliquely, and then the Equator between 23° and 28° W. long., and take one of the routes previously indicated, either to the western coast of Africa or the eastern coast of America. In treating of the routes from the coast of Africa to the ports of North America, that from the Cape of Good Hope to these ports need only be pointed out, from which the rest may be easily deduced.

Leaving the Cape between October and April the prevailing winds will be found from S.E., and the course will be the same as that previously shown for returning to Europe until the Equator is crossed in

28° W. From thence a vessel would pass West of the shoal called Penedo de St. Pedro, and proceed with the Trade winds from East or E.N.E. in order to pass at a good distance to windward of the Lesser Antilles. This course, as may have been seen, presents no difficulty.

A ship rounding the Cape of Good Hope between the months of March and September, should avoid the coast on account of the N.W. winds, which blow with violence during the winter, and keep South of the zone of the Trade winds in order to reach the parallel of 20° S. lat. in the meridian of 18° W. She would then steer northward and cross the line in 33° W. long. During this season it is preferable to cross the Equator on this meridian rather than in a more eastern one. It is also better to pass East of the Bermudas if she should be bound to a port of Nova Scotia, instead of West of them, because at this period easterly winds are often found in those parts. The rule generally adopted is to pass East of the Bermudas from the middle of March till October in going to any port on the coast of North America situated North of New York.

From the different routes now pointed out it will be easy to design any that may be required from one point to another of the Atlantic Ocean.

CHAPTER XI.

Concluding general Views on making Passages in the Atlantic.

The principles to be observed in making a passage between two places, whether under sail only or with the assistance of steam, are:—1.—Never to hug the wind when it is foul, but to let the ship go at least a point free through the water; and, 2.—To profit as much as possible by the well-known prevailing currents of the several seas, that are happily so distributed throughout them, as to be favourable for the navigator in different latitudes when he is desirous of reaching either shore from any place, whether this be on the same or on the opposite coast; and 3.—To lay the ship's head on that tack, with a foul wind, that will enable her to look best up for her port.

All currents are more or less influenced by the wind. Before, therefore, commencing with the mode of making passages, it may be as well to take a rapid view of the prevailing winds which are to regulate the seaman's course from port to port.

Within the tropics the prevailing wind is generally easterly; to the northward of the Equator as well as to the southward of it, it draws slightly towards either pole according as the sun retires from it. Those winds, called the Trade winds, prevail throughout the Equatorial regions of the Atlantic and Pacific Oceans; but in the Indian Ocean they are modified by the proximity of the great continents—by which their character is totally changed; and according to the position of the sun (as they generally blow towards it) they become monsoons or periodical winds, but still subject to certain modifications.

The extensive space between the tropics and either pole is the region of the variable winds; generally assuming a contrary direction to the Trade winds, to contribute, perhaps, with other phenomena to preserve the atmospheric equilibrium or counterpoise that is found in all the operations of nature. But the whole subject of atmospheric changes, like that of natural history generally, is replete with these beneficial arrangements of an all-wise Creator in anticipation of the wants of his creature man to reach readily the different parts of the globe which he inhabits, by the aid of navigation. So that he may turn to his account the winds and the currents which again and again change their directions with the seasons of the year. All is ceaseless change, perpetually working to his good.

Such is the reflection resulting from a general view of the winds; their several peculiar modifications will appear as we proceed and have to allude to them in showing the manner of making the several passages on which we propose to treat.

A ship leaving the British Channel for any port to

the southward should first gain a good offing, and then shape her course according to the wind, modifying it according to that which may be expected as she proceeds. In crossing the Bay of Biscay much will depend on the direction of the wind and how it has previously been. If it has been to the northward of West the Rennel current is somewhat checked, and occasionally the set is found to be to the westward, along the North coast of Spain, and thence off Cape Finisterre to the S.W., eventually joining the Portugal current running to the southward. Again, if the wind be to the southward of West the strength of the Rennel current is considerably increased, causing a strong indraught into the bay,

There is little doubt that the lamentable wreck of *H.M.S. Serpent* in November 1890, near Cape Villano, was due to an increased strength of this set caused by strong westerly winds. The *S.S. Wordsworth*, which crossed the bay at the same time, was found to be, when observations were first obtained, in the latitude of Madeira, 50 miles East of her dead reckoning.

A vessel bound to a port on the Spanish coast in the bay should, therefore, endeavour to make the land to the eastward or westward of it according as she may have had the wind, so as to make the land to windward of that port. But for a vessel bound to the southward of Cape Finisterre a S.W. course is recommended in order to reach fine weather as soon as possible. And having gained the latitude of 45°, should the vessel be bound to Oporto or Lisbon, it might be well to make the land about Cape Torinaña, as by route A, and close with it if going to the former port. If to the latter, the vessel will make the best progress she can to the southward with a good offing of 30 to 60 miles from the coast, and make the Rock of Lisbon, from whence she will gain her port. If bound to Gibraltar or up the Strait she will still be in a good position for that destination. The passage from the Channel to Lisbon or the Straits will vary from four or five days to a week or more, depending much on the direction of the wind.

In the case, however, of a vessel bound southward, as soon as she has reached the parallel of 45° in about 12° West, she would shape her course direct for Madeira, as by route B, or if not desiring to touch there, for the Canary Islands. In case of going to Madeira, Porto Santo should be made, and from thence the East end of the island will be passed and Funchal Roads will be gained.

In the winter months it is preferable to pass round the West side of Madeira, as heavy squalls at that time are frequently experienced on the East side of the island.

In the case of a vessel stopping at the Canaries, she will probably round Point Anaga, and anchor off Santa Cruz. The anchorage off Palma is preferred to that of Santa Cruz, as having, it is said, more resources and being easy to leave, while the latter anchorage is much exposed to S.E. winds, and is not so easily left as Palma. But if it be not desired by a vessel to touch at any place on her way southward she may continue her course, passing to the East or West of these islands, and reach the Trade wind as soon as she can. She will generally be more certain of a breeze by passing to the westward of the islands. The passage to Madeira from the Channel is considered to occupy about a week or ten days.

Continuing her progress to the southward on the eastern side of the Atlantic, should a vessel be going to the coast of Africa, the Cape Verd Islands may be her next place of call, for which a S.W. course will be proper. In this route there is nothing to observe upon further than that she has more chance of a breeze by keeping her distance from the coast. In June the passage inside the Cape Verd Islands may be taken, on the meridian of 20° W., with advantage.

If bound to the Gambia or Sierra Leone, whether from the Cape Verds or the Canary Group, the ship would endeavour to make Cape Verd as by the inner route C, from whence she would have the current and wind in her favour, and make the land to windward of her port. From either of these places, if required, the route to any part of the coast is easy by keeping within the limits of the easterly current, the shortest distance of which from the coast is about 70 miles off Cape Palmas; and in this manner, by keeping in this Guinea current along the shore, as in route D, or the westerly current in the offing outside of it, passages are made to and from ports as far as Fernando Po and Princes and St. Thomas Islands. But to the southward of those ports to reach places on the coast, as the prevailing wind all the year is between S.W. and S.S.E., then a ship must get to the southward of her destined port with a good offing, and allow for a northerly current also, while she is standing in for the coast on the starboard tack, taking care always to make it to the southward or windward of the port to which she is proceeding. And this observation refers to the whole extent of the coast to the southward, but as the Cape is approached, N.W. or S.W. and even S.E. winds will be mostly found, the latter especially being very strong.

A vessel bound to Ascension from the Canary Islands from November to February inclusive, would do well to make good a course so that she would pass about midway between the Cape Verd Islands and the coast, as in the inner route C. Passing these islands she might with advantage avail herself of the Guinea current to help her down to the N.E. of that island, along route D, and would thence stand across the Equatorial current to the southward and make Ascension with the S.E. Trade. If bound to St. Helena from thence, she must stand on across the Trade and get into the zone of the variable westerly winds to the southward of its latitude, as shown by route E, and navigate so as to reach to the S.E. of the island, from whence she would run down to it with the prevailing S.E. winds. But in the other months, a ship bound to Ascension or St. Helena might do better by taking the route C across the Equator in about 20°, and standing to the southward to about 15° S., so as to be able to lay some points to windward of it with the S.E. Trade, making it with a fair wind from the southward. And in the same manner St. Helena would be gained, as shown from the route C or that of E from Ascension.

A vessel bound to the Cape should make the best of her way to the southward by routes B and C, which will take her as far as the Cape Verd Islands. From thence she would cross the Equator in 25° to 30° West, according to the season, as already pointed out, standing across the S.E. Trade, and making the best of her way to the zone of the variables, crossing the parallel of 30° S. in about 15° to 20° West (see route F), where she will meet westerly winds, with which she will soon reach the Cape. This passage has been made to the eastward, but the S.W. winds near the coast are so heavy as well as unfavourable that a vessel is unable to make so good a passage as by the route here pointed out.

Returning home from the Cape a vessel may shape her course by the route L, which will take her by St. Helena and Ascension, from whence she may cross the Equator in from 20° to 30° W., and follow that route to the northward as the wind may permit, observing the maxim with which we set out, of letting the ship make her way a point free from the wind.

Passages to the western ports of the Atlantic from the Channel vary as to the mode of making them according to their position. Thus to ports of Nova Scotia, Newfoundland, or the St. Lawrence, the nearest distance is by the northern route G, making good as far as 53° N. latitude, and then, as the coast is approached, there is the chance of making it with

N.W. winds; while by standing to the southward at first, the whole force of the Gulf Stream current has to be met. But in shaping her course with a contrary wind, a ship should adopt that tack on which she will make most westing.

In crossing the Atlantic for any of the western ports, there are few months of the year in which a vessel may not expect to meet with ice. Happily the sea is less encumbered with it in the dark nights of winter than in summer, when there is so much more daylight that it is less difficult to avoid. Drifting down from the shores of Greenland and Labrador, it is most commonly found in the Atlantic in the earliest part of our summer, and lingering far to the eastward to the last days of our autumnal quarter. But it is most abundant near the banks of Newfoundland. Between the Virgin Rocks and Newfoundland the ice completely lines the coast in the severity of winter, and is succeeded in the spring by the drift ice on which the seal fishery is followed. Eastward of the banks the commonly assigned limits to their dangers are 40° W. long. and 40° N. lat., see x on the chart. In some instances ice has been met with far to the eastward of this position, and therefore having commenced the passage across the Atlantic, whether by the northern or southern route, the most vigilant look out is required to avoid running into it.

The routes for steamers bound to and from North America, which were recommended by Lieut. Maury, have been adopted by some of the Atlantic Lines. He proposed that the northern track should be taken by vessels from Europe to America, and the other, about 60 miles to the southward, should be followed by those from America to Europe; a judicious arrangement, by which those vessels going West are less within the effects of the Gulf Stream, while those from the westward are always in a position to profit most by it, and the risk of collision is considerably lessened.

A vessel bound to Halifax, following up the route G, will endeavour to make the land to the southward of her port, where a remarkable distinguishing feature, alluded to in the directions, enables her to recognize it, and thence how to approach it: but in making for New York or any port of the States, she will ascertain by her thermometer when she is crossing the Gulf Stream. Nor must her commander be surprised at passing two distinct currents of warm water, having done which he will find a counter-current setting to the southward along the American coast. But in making the passage it is recommended not to pass to the northward of Sable Island, in order to avoid being set down by the tides into the bay formed by its two extremes slightly curving as they do to the northward. The passage to Halifax may occupy 30 or 35 days, while that to New York takes from 36 to 40 days to perform; the return passages to the Channel generally requiring less.

A vessel bound to any of the West India Islands or ports of the continent within them, should make her way to the S.W., so as to pick up the Trades near Madeira. She may probably have to touch at that island. But she will find the Trade wind earlier or later when in its neighbourhood according as the sun has northern or southern declination. And she will make the best of her way to the S.W., shaping her course according to the southern or northern position of the island to which she is bound, as shown by the routes H and J. But if between May and December, she should keep as much as she can along the parallel of 19° N., and if between December and June, she should keep further South, taking care to make due allowance for the current, which will always place her ahead of her position by the reckoning, and will at least amount to about 12 miles per day. If bound to any of the large islands or the coast of Mexico, she would enter the Caribbean Sea between Martinique and Antigua, by route H, or if to Cartagena or Porto Bello, she would pass on either side of St. Lucia, and fall into route K. Again, if bound to either of the ports of Guiana or Venezuela, she would shape her course by route K, so as to make the land well to the eastward of her port; taking care that she is not drifted past it by the current, which will be found to acquire strength as she nears the coast. But to do this a vessel should stand South across the N.E. Trade and the variables, so as to reach the S.E. Trade and edge away to the coast according to the position of her port.

A vessel homeward bound from the West Indies would adopt the eastern route O, or the western ones M or N by the Florida Stream, according as she is to windward or to leeward. Thus from St. Thomas or any of the Caribbee Islands, she would stand to the northward by adopting nearly the route N. If from Jamaica, she may either pass between St. Domingo and Cuba, along the old Bahama Channel, North of Cuba, or run to leeward round its western end and pass Havana up the Florida Channel by the route M. This is obviously the homeward route for vessels from the Gulf of Mexico, while those from Guayana and Venezuela may adopt the route N, those from the latter gaining it by passing through the Mona Passage between St. Domingo and Porto Rico, or they may take that between Cuba and St. Domingo, and thence join the route M.

It has been observed by an officer of considerable experience in West India cruising that the probable best homeward route from Jamaica is by the windward passage between St. Domingo and Cuba, thence by the Crooked Island Channel to the N.E., thus joining the route N. This is best adapted, however, to smart sailing ships; but that most generally adopted especially when so far to leeward as Jamaica, is to run westward round the West end of Cuba, and so up to the northward with the Gulf Stream, by the route M.

A vessel bound to any port of the northern coast of Brazil, will adopt the route K or F as far as the Equator, from whence she would shape her course so as to be on the coast well to the eastward of the port to which she is bound, and be careful not to be set to the westward of it by the current. A vessel bound to Pernambuco or Bahia will equally observe the route F as far as the Equator, always making the land to the northward of either of those ports, and allowing for the Brazil current, which runs along the coast from Cape San Roque to the southward. From October to March, when the sun is to the southward, the wind is directly on shore, and the current sets to the southward; but from March to October the current inshore sets northerly.

A vessel bound to Rio or Buenos Ayres will continue on her route F, and approaching the coast gradually, will make it about Cape Frio, by which she will have all the advantage of the Brazil current. On leaving any of these ports for Europe, a vessel has to gain if she can the homeward route L, or to cross the Equator as near it as she can, and gain it as she can, although she may not be able to do so even as far North as 30° lat. But to reach a port on the opposite coast of Africa, it is obvious that her proceedings must depend on the latitude of the port which she is leaving as well as that to which she would proceed. It is clear that on any part of the Brazil coast she is dead to leeward of her destination, and she has to cross the Atlantic to the southward or the northward, as most favourable to her.

The passage from Rio to the Cape is sufficiently favourable. A vessel will stand to the S.E., as on route P, and soon find variable winds, and as she makes southing along with her easting will pick up westerly winds, which will speedily carry her to the Cape on this route; and vessels from Bahia and Pernambuco for the Cape would follow a similar course, first not being afraid of making southing. In fact, having gained the region of southerly and S.S.W. winds between 20° and 30° S., a vessel may run in upon any part of the African coast that she requires to make. But if she be to the northward of Pernambuco, or even at Cape St. Roque, she must make the best of her way across the Trade to the northward, making a detour, and reaching as high, perhaps, as the latitude of Madeira till she finds the variables, in which she may make her easting, and thence run down and take any port she may require on the coast by the route C already mentioned. Vessels from the African coast coming to the coast of Brazil, and desiring to return, should keep to the southward of Cape St. Roque, as the return passage from thence is incomparably shorter to the southward of the S.E. Trade than to the northward of the N.E. Trade, especially when the sun is to the North of the Equator.

It is to be observed that the several routes delineated on the chart, and here referred to, are those expressing approximately the tracks which ships are recommended to follow. But as their ability to do this will much depend on the wind that they may severally meet with, the various routes must be considered as merely meant for their guidance, to be followed as nearly as the winds will admit.

BRITISH
19 SE 94
MUSEUM

INDEX.

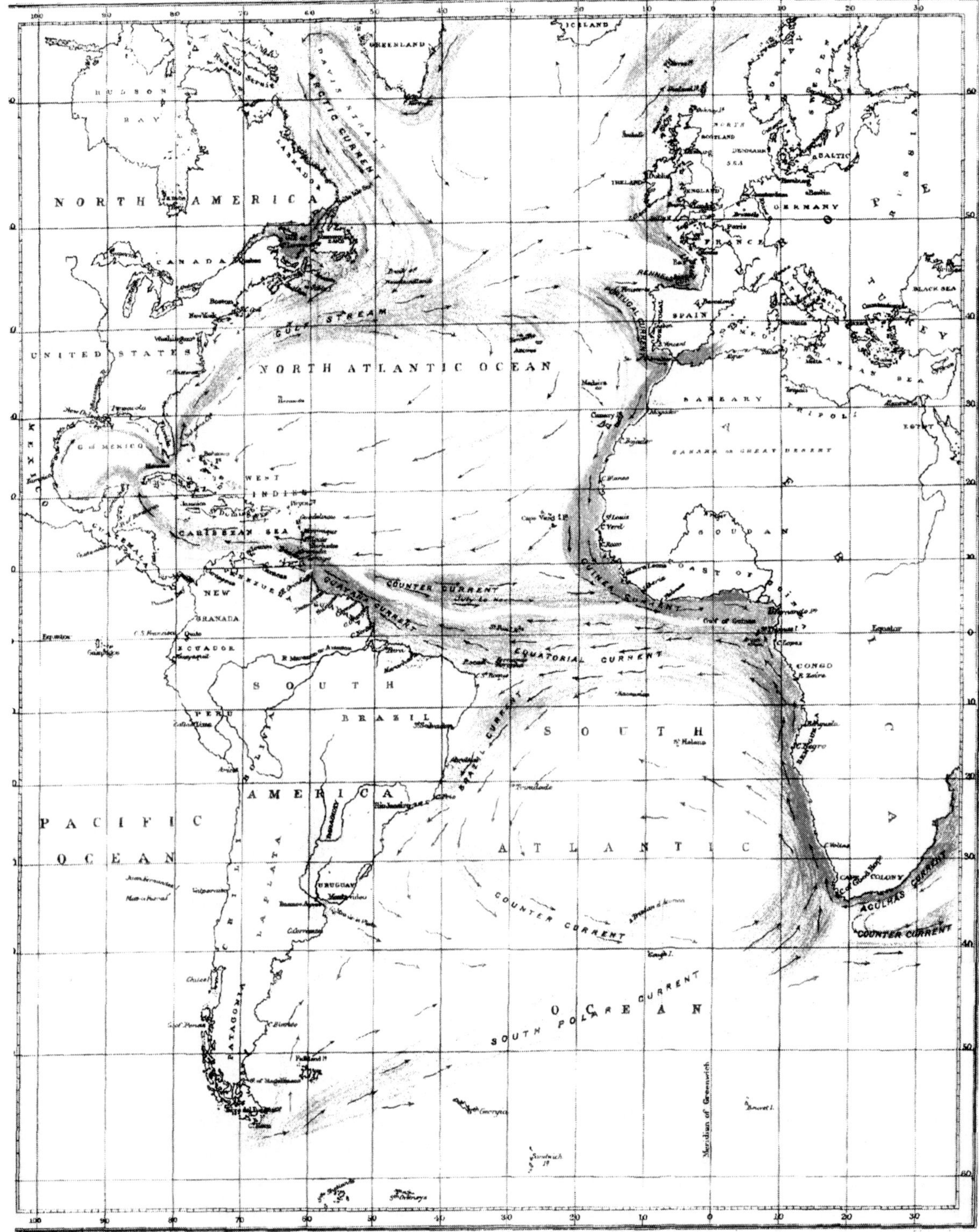
NORTH AMERICA
HUDSON BAY
CANADA
UNITED STATES
GREENLAND
ICELAND
DAVIS STRAIT
ARCTIC CURRENT
GULF STREAM
NORTH ATLANTIC OCEAN
G. of MEXICO
CARIBBEAN SEA
WEST INDIES
NEW GRANADA
ECUADOR
COUNTER CURRENT
GUIANA CURRENT
EQUATORIAL CURRENT
GUINEA CURRENT
SOUTH AMERICA
BRAZIL
BRAZIL CURRENT
PERU
BOLIVIA
CHILI
LA PLATA
URUGUAY
PATAGONIA
PACIFIC OCEAN
SOUTH ATLANTIC
COUNTER CURRENT
SOUTH POLAR CURRENT
SOUTH OCEAN
AGULHAS CURRENT
COUNTER CURRENT
CAPE COLONY
CONGO
SOUDAN
COAST OF GUINEA
SAHARA or GREAT DESERT
BARBARY
SPAIN
FRANCE
GERMANY
ENGLAND
IRELAND
SCOTLAND
NORTH SEA
BALTIC
DENMARK
TURKEY
BLACK SEA
EGYPT
EUROPE
AFRICA
Meridian of Greenwich

BRITISH
10 SE 94
MUSEUM

NORTH AMERICA
UNITED STATES
CANADA
MEXICO
NORTH ATLANTIC OCEAN
ROUTE G
ROUTE M
ROUTE N
ROUTE H
ROUTE L
ROUTE K
ROUTE C
ROUTE D
ROUTE F
ROUTE P
Region of prevailing West Winds
Region of the N.E. Trade Winds
Zone of Equatorial variable Winds
Region of the South East Trade Winds
Mean Limit of S.E. Trade
Region of prevailing Westerly Winds
WEST INDIES
CARIBBEAN SEA
NEW GRANADA
ECUADOR
PERU
BRAZIL
SOUTH AMERICA
CHILI
LA PLATA
URUGUAY
PATAGONIA
PACIFIC OCEAN
SOUTH ATLANTIC OCEAN
EUROPE
RUSSIA
GERMANY
FRANCE
SPAIN
IRELAND
ENGLAND
SWEDEN
NORWAY
BALTIC
TURKEY
BLACK SEA
BARBARY
TRIPOLI
EGYPT
SAHARA or GREAT DESERT
SOUDAN
AFRICA
CONGO
CAPE COLONY
ICELAND
GREENLAND
HUDSON BAY
TO AUSTRALIA
Equator
Meridian of Greenwich
J.D. Potter London

	s.	d.
Admiralty Procedure against Merchant Ships and Cargoes, &c., by *R. G. M. Browne*, the Admiralty Marshal	10	0
The Statute Law of Merchant Shipping, comprised in an alphabetical analysis, and a Summary of the unrepealed Merchant Shipping Acts, from 1821 to 1888, by *R. G. M. Browne*, the Admiralty Marshal	6	0
An Essay on Hydrographical Engineering, as applicable to Floating Sea Barriers, Harbours, Batteries, Coast Defences, and Naval Fortifications, by *Capt. Adderley Sleigh, K.T.S., F.R.S.L.* (with Illustrations), 1859	10	0
Pilot's Handbook for the English Channel, by *Capt. King, R.N.*	7	6
Foreign Measures and their English Values, compiled from Official Sources, by *R. C. Carrington, F.R.G.S.*	7	6
Tables showing the Length in Feet of a Degree, Minute, and Second of Latitude and Longitude, with the corresponding number of Statute Miles in each Degree of Latitude; and the number of Minutes of Latitude or Nautic Miles contained in a Degree of Longitude, under each Parallel of Latitude, by *R. C. Carrington, F.R.G.S.*	1	0
Elementary Manual for the Deviations of the Compass in Iron Ships, by *Capt. F. J. Evans, R.N.*	6	6
Tide Charts of the English and Bristol Channels and Entrance of the Thames, compiled from the Admiralty Tide Tables, by *Algernon Heber Percy*, late Lieut. Royal Navy	5	0
The A.B.C. of Sumner's Method of ascertaining a Ship's Position by Projection, by *Digby Murray*	5	0
Notes on the Management of Chronometers and the Measurement of Meridian Distances, by *Rear-Admiral Charles Shadwell, C.B., F.R.S.*	4	6
Tables for Facilitating the Reduction of Lunar Observations, by *Rear-Admiral Charles Shadwell, C.B., F.R.S.*	4	6
Formulæ of Navigation and Nautical Astronomy do.	2	6
Tables for Facilitating the Determination of the Latitude and Time at Sea by Observations of the Stars, by *Rear-Admiral Charles Shadwell, C.B., F.R.S.* ..	2	6
Notes on Interpolation, Mathematical and Practical do.	2	0
Chart of the Navy of Great Britain, from the Earliest Period of History, compiled from historical publications, old records, parliamentary returns, and other authorities, by *Frederick Perigal* (*of the Admiralty*), 1860	3	6
An Introduction to the Practice of Navigation and Nautical Astronomy, by *R. E. Hooppell, M.A., F.R.A.S.*	3	6
Hour Angles of the Sun, Moon, and Stars, for Latitude and Declination 0°-80°, and Altitude 5°-64°, together with Short Methods of finding the Longitude by Chronometer; and the Latitude and Longitude by Two "Chronometers," by *A. C. Johnson, R.N.*	3	6
Short Tables and Rules for Finding Latitude and Longitude do.	3	0
How to Find the Time at Sea in Less than a Minute, being a New and Accurate Method with specially adapted Tables, by *A. C. Johnson, R.N.*	2	6
Combined Time and Altitude Azimuth Tables for all Latitudes and Declinations, by *A. C. Johnson, R.N.*	2	6
Finding the Latitude and Longitude in Cloudy Weather, by *A. C. Johnson, R.N.* ..	1	0
Practical Information on the Deviation of the Compass, for the use of Masters and Mates of Iron Ships, by *J. T. Towson, F.R.G.S.*	4	0
Tables for the Reduction of Ex-meridian Altitudes, by *J. T. Towson, F.R.G.S.* ..	1	0
An Elementary Treatise on the Tides, based upon that of the late Sir J. W. Lubbock, Bart., F.R.S., to which is added a newly-devised method of computation of the heights of high water at Liverpool, with factors for other ports and tables adopted by the Admiralty, by *James Pearson, M.A., F.R.A.S.*	3	6
The true principle of the Law of Storms, practically arranged for both Hemispheres, by *James Sedgwick*	3	0
A Chart of South Latitudes, beyond 20 degrees, to facilitate the practice of Great Circle Sailing; with an accompanying Diagram for the determination of the Courses and Distances, by *Hugh Godfray, M.A.*	3	0
Time Azimuth Diagram, by *Hugh Godfray, M.A.*	3	0

	s.	d.
Captain Weir's Azimuth Diagram	1	6
Practical Nautical Surveying (a lecture delivered at the Royal United Service Institution, 1872), by *Staff Commander Thomas A. Hull, R.N.*	3	0
Observations on the Rule of the Road at Sea, prepared for and dedicated to Officers and Seamen of the Mercantile Marine, by *Thomas Gray*	2	0
"Going to Sea," or "Under the Red Ensign," a plain guide to Parents, Guardians, and Boys, by *Thomas Gray*	1	0
Remarks on Rigging Ships with Flat Surface Sails, by *Lieut. William Congalton, R.N.R.*	2	0
On the Stability of Ships and Floating Bodies, by *Alf. J. Cooper* (Master Mariner) ..	1	6
Seamanship and Navigation, Required for the Ordinary Examination, by *Capt. R. Maxwell* .. .. 1s., and Cloth	1	6
Seamanship and Navigation, Required for the Extra Master's Examination, by *Capt. R. Maxwell* .. .. 1s., and Cloth	1	6
A Review of the New Methods of Lowering and Disconnecting Boats at Sea, with a Proposed Amendment (1857), by *Capt. Kynaston, R.N., C.B., &c.*	1	6
Speed Tables, for finding the distance run in a given time at a given speed, between the limits of 10 to 18 Knots, by *J. D. Macpherson* (Pacific Steam Navigation Co.)	1	0
Pole-Star Latitude: a Method of finding the Latitude from an Altitude of the Pole-Star, by *Darnton Hutton* (Master Mariner), *B.A., M. Inst. C.E.*	1	0
General Guide to Marine Insurance, by *J. P. Godfrey*	1	0
Handbook on the Law and Practise relating to Apprentices to the Mercantile Marine Service, by *F. W. Gardner* (of the Middle Temple)	1	0
A Voice from the Quarter-Deck on the State of our Mercantile Marine, by *Joseph Mayne* (Master Mariner)	1	0
How Ships are Lost, and How to Save Life and Property at Sea (Illustrated), by *W. P. B. Manser*	1	0
A Method for Finding the Latitude by the Simultaneous Altitudes of Two Stars, by *Capt. Burdwood, R.N.*	1	0
Ship's Cook and Steward's Guide, containing Hints for Management, and two hundred and fifty recipes, by *James B. Wilson*	1	0
Historical Notes on Shipping, by *P. L. Isaac (Member of the Institution of Naval Architects)*	1	0
Dock Pass Book	1	0
Lights in Lyrics, or a Glance at the Channel Lights as Piloting Marks, on a run from Scilly to the Nore, accompanied by a parting precept on Compass Deviation, addressed to all younger Mariners (with a view of the Caskets), Notes and Chart, 1859	1	0
Swinging Ship for Deviation (Board of Trade, 1859), compiled by *Rear-Admiral Fitzroy, F.R.S.*	1	0
A Review of the Proceedings of the Arctic Searching Expeditions, under the command of Capt. H. T. Austin, C.B., and Capt. Wm. Penny (with a Chart), 1851	1	0
Ditto ditto Arctic Papers No. 2 (1851)	0	6
Ditto ditto ditto No. 3 (1852)	0	6
The Arctic Dispatches, containing an Account of the Discovery of the North-West Passage by Capt. Robert Maclure (commanding H.M.S. "Investigator"), with a Map of the Discoveries in the Arctic Regions, 1852-3	2	0
The True Direction and Velocity of Wind, observed from Ships while Sailing, by *James N. Miller* (Member of the Liverpool Polytechnic Society), with Table for Indicating the True Direction of Winds at Sea, 1870	0	6
Navigation, intended for Self-instruction up to the Second Mate's Examination, by *William Roy*	0	6
An Address delivered to the Boys of the Training Ships "Chichester" and the "Arethusa," by *G. M. Coxhead*	0	4

ADMIRALTY INDEX CHARTS.

PRICE 6d. EACH.

The Admiralty Chart Index Sheets will be found very useful to Captains in their selection of Charts.

A—The World. B—England, Ireland, and Channel Islands. C—Scotland. D—North, Baltic, and White Seas. E—France, Spain, Portugal, and the Mediterranean Sea. F—Africa and adjacent Islands. G—Indian Ocean. H—Western Australia and Eastern Archipelago. I—East Australia and New Zealand. J—China Sea, Siam, and Phillipine Islands to Japan. K—Japan Islands, Korea, and Manchuria. L—Islands in the Pacific Ocean. M—West Coast of North America. N—South America. O—West Indies and Central America. P—East Coast of North America.

171. Index Chart of Admiralty Sailing Directions.

Signs and Abbreviations adopted in the Admiralty Charts, 6d.

Official Catalogue of Charts, Plans, and Sailing Directions, 1s.

Prices for Mounting (on Linen) the Admiralty Charts:—	*s.*	*d.*
Small Sheet, 20 × 27 in.	1	0
Large Sheet, 40 × 27 in.	1	6
Larger Sheets than above.. .. .. 2/- and	2	6

Leather Portfolios and Index (size 27½ × 21½ × 4 in.) with straps and buckles, for the Admiralty Charts, 20/- each.

POTTER'S NAUTICAL ACADEMY,

11, KING STREET, TOWER HILL, LONDON,

Conducted by CAPTAIN R. MAXWELL.

Captains and Officers of the Merchant Service prepared to pass the Local Marine Board Examinations, both in NAVIGATION and SEAMANSHIP.

Also a complete course of Navigation, Trigonometry, &c., taught on moderate terms.

CAPT. R. MAXWELL has passed his Examinations (Ordinary and Extra) at the LONDON LOCAL MARINE BOARD, and has conducted the above Academy since the year 1867.

CPSIA information can be obtained at www.ICGtesting.com
Printed in the USA
LVOW111518280413

331279LV00011B/137/P